BMW K-SERIES MOTORCYCLES

BMW K-SERIES MOTORCYCLES

MICK WALKER & PETER DOBSON

Foulis

Haynes
®

A **FOULIS** Motorcycling Book

First published 1989

© **Mick Walker and
Peter Dobson 1989**

Published by:
**Haynes Publishing Group
Sparkford, Nr. Yeovil,
Somerset BA22 7JJ, England.**

**Haynes Publications Inc.
861 Lawrence Drive, Newbury
Park, California 91320, USA.**

British Library Cataloguing in
Publication data
Walker, Mick
BMW K-Series Motorcycles.
(General Motorcycling).
1. BMW Motorcycles to 1988
I. Title   II. Dobson, Peter.
III. Series,
629.2'275
ISBN 0-85429-724-3

Library of Congress catalog card
number **88-082501**

Editor: **Robin Read**
Design and layout: **Mike King**
Printed in England by:
J.H. Haynes & Co. Ltd.

Contents

B M W _____ K Series

Introduction & Acknowledgments

The idea for this book came about by chance, following a casual conversation with Arthur Dalziel, former Motorcycle Sales Manager of BMW GB Ltd.

Collecting a road test machine from the company's headquarters at Bracknell, Berkshire, I raised with him the possibility of a marque history of BMW for *Motorcycle Enthusiast* magazine. Arthur said that, in his opinion, it would be more interesting to trace the development of the new K-Series bikes for there were already lots of articles and several books about the 'boxer' twins.

That was in 1985. Two years and several road tests later I had covered many miles on the entire K-series range and had realised that I just had to write a book about them for I had become genuinely enthusiastic about these unique machines.

As a one time road racer, dealer and importer, as well as being a former editor of *MCE*, I have sampled hundreds of machines over a quarter of a century, including all the latest hardware from Japan and feel qualified to comment with some authority upon the products of the motorcycle industry.

There is a vast number of motorcycles currently on offer and it is possible to purchase one that will fulfil almost any specialised requirement. But it is much more difficult to find one that will fulfil several different roles with ease.

It is here that the BMW K-Series comes into its own. They may not be the fastest, the best handling, the most economical or the best looking machines around but, unlike most modern bikes, the K-Series BMWs are equally at home trickling through heavy traffic on congested city streets; cruising down a Continental autobahn at well over 100mph; or even competing in an international road race for production sports machines. Quite simply, the threes and fours from Spandau are at the very top of any chart awarding points for versatility.

Of course – and I have not pulled any punches here – the Ks have had their problems, particularly in the early days. And although the current models are exceedingly reliable, it goes to show that even BMW do not always get it right first time.

But, at least in concept, the factory got it right. And as evidence of this belief I am the owner of an K75S, paid for with my own hard-earned cash, in case anyone should think it was a present from a grateful company. Not only have they managed to retain as customers the great majority of BMW enthusiasts but, with the help of clever advertising in up-market general interest magazines, they have appealed to a status-conscious group that BMW call ALBs, or 'Affluent Lapsed Bikers', and brought them back into the fold to buy and ride a BMW in addition to attracting less well-heeled, more dedicated, buyers.

I have never previously owned a BMW but I could compile a lengthy list of British, Italian and even Japanese machinery that I have purchased. Years ago I did aspire to an R69S twin, which was too expensive, but I now regard the 'boxers' as being obsolete, although some enthusiastic owners might prefer to think of them as 'Classic'.

As a recent convert to the marque I have noticed a strange tendency amongst the owners of machines that do not have horizontal engines to tell me, at some length, why I should not own a BMW. In fact, I experienced this odd phenomenon in 1983 when I had a 'boxer' twin for road test. The owner of a Vincent V-twin stopped especially to criticise what he thought was my machine. It was quite funny, really. When he had run out of abuse the Vincent would not start again, while I pressed the starter button and purred off, smugly, on the BMW.

The feeling that the product cannot possibly match up to the glossy image cultivated by BMW's publicity machine could be behind this disapproval. Certainly the company take Public Relations very seriously and, compared to other manufacturers, they really cannot be faulted for the steady flow of press releases, photographs, brochures, general information and road test bikes. The corporate body that is BMW today is geared to publicity. But it must be good publicity, of course. And while the staff of BMW GB are always helpfulness itself, not one hint of criticism of the product has escaped from Bracknell. Blank looks were the response to any mention of the well authenticated problems of the early versions of the fours and threes and I have consulted owners, dealers and mechanics involved with the K-Series to hear the other side and to present a balanced view.

The dealers – and their staff – expressed a preference for anonymity but I extend my gratitude to them for all their help and kindness. Of those that I can mention, Doug Jackson of the World's Motorcycles News Agency has, as in earlier titles, provided photographs and a wealth of useful information from his world-wide contacts. My thanks must also go to Nick Jeffries for relating his experiences when racing K100RS in the Production Tourist Trophy race in the Isle of Man; to Fred Secker, past president of the British arm of the BMW Owners Club, for offering encouragement and kindly reading through the manuscript; and Lorna Arnold and Chris Willows, of BMW GB's PR department, for their kindness and their prompt attention to requests for photographs and information.

I should like to thank my old friend Robin Read for providing the spark which was to ignite into the completed manuscript. And finally my co-author Peter Dobson.

My appreciation and gratitude goes to Classic racer and BMW

Mick Walker pictured with a K100RS at Donington Park 23 July 1987, when he was able to sample the entire BMW range in a single day.

K-Series line-up as it was in the Summer of 1986.

K100RS owner Mick White for providing his own experiences of long term ownership, which gives unique insight and provides the text with additional authority.

BMW K-Series Motorcycles sets out to record how these remarkable machines came to complement so successfully the famous, much loved and long running twins. And delves behind the glamour of the advertising to find out just what these bikes are like to ride and own. Here, then, is the story for existing owners and potential purchasers alike.

Mick Walker
Wisbech, Cambridgeshire

DECEMBER 1988

Foreword

I am privileged to have been asked by Mick Walker and Peter Dobson to write the foreword to their book on the BMW 'K' Series motorcycles.

I have also been privileged to have been Motorcycle Manager at BMW (GB) Ltd during the world launch of the 'K' and its most exciting and successful introduction into the British motorcycle market.

We were often asked when the 'K' Series arrived why, when we enjoyed the reputation for building traditional motorcycles of quality and to a high standard, did we decide to produce a completely new machine after 60 years of 'Boxer' domination?

– by Pat Myers
(Motorcycle Manager
BMW [GB] Ltd)

The answer must lie in our belief that we could produce a new motorcycle which would be not only different but even better and further enhance our reputation. There is no doubt that the range epitomises the age of advanced technology, with electronic controls and computer aided design; up to date aerodynamic styling and the very latest production techniques which, at the 'K's' inception, were world firsts. Development naturally continues with the introduction of the ABS braking system for instance, and the other exciting developments planned.

It is remarkable how since its launch the 'K' Series has fitted into the overall range of models and, although the 'K' is now in the ascendancy as far as sales are concerned, it runs happily alongside our 'Boxer' models with each Series complementing the other.

Whenever we talk about the development of the 'K' it is natural that our thoughts turn to that quiet, unassuming, friendly Austrian Stefan Pachernegg, the brilliant engineer mainly responsible for the later development work on the 'K' Series. His sudden death at the age of 43 from a heart attack in Paris in February 1987 was a truly tragic loss not only to BMW Motorrad, but also to his many friends.

Congratulations to Mick Walker and Peter Dobson for their excellent and interesting book and I know they will agree with me it chronicles only the beginning of the story.

Before the K—The First Sixty Years

BMW AG are undoubtedly a great success. Their cars are like a uniform amongst the status-conscious. As Germany's last large volume motorcycle manufacturer, their products sell extremely well in a generally unhappy market and they have a solid reputation both for sound design and engineering. The company has had a name for quality since its early days but they have never been so good at marketing as they are today. Circumstances have also conspired against them and on one or two occasions BMW has come close to bankruptcy.

As a manufacturer of motorcars BMW's beginnings go back to 1896 when an industrialist named Heinrich Erhart opened a factory at Eisenach intending to make military equipment but, instead, he switched to building shaft-drive bicycles and electrically powered vehicles. After four years the far sighted Heinrich could clearly see that the commercial possibilities were somewhat limited and he went over to producing Decauville cars – which he called Wartburgs – under licence from the French factory.

Erhart soon moved on, leaving his son to continue building cars, albeit in another factory, while the Eisenach plant was taken over by a new company formed by several of the restless Erhart's former colleagues. They began to build a range of cars intended to appeal to the nobility and gentry under the unlikely name of Dixi but, presumably, with some success as they were still there in 1928 when BMW bought them out.

Another component part of BMW was formed, unwittingly, in 1911 when Gustav Otto, son of the famous Nikolaus August Otto, creator of the four-stroke engine, set up an aircraft company with the resounding title of the Gustav Otto Flugmaschinenfabrik München – which simply meant that they made aeroplanes in Munich – in a factory on the Lerchenauerstrasse at the eastern end of the Oberweisenfeld Airport, a site still occupied by BMW's headquarters.

The third unknowing antecedent was the Rapp Motorenwerke GmbH, formed by Karl Rapp in 1913 to profit from the coming war by making aero engines. An important step towards the formation of the present company took place on 7 March, 1916 when Karl Rapp and Dr Ing E Max Friz, a designer of aero engines, combined their talents under the name of Bayerische Flugzeugwerke AG, or BFW.

They were the new firm's two directors and they concentrated all their efforts and resources on the manufacturing of aircraft engines to such effect that their main consumers, the front-line pilots of the German air force, were lavish in their praise. The legendary Baron Manfred von Richthofen was especially appreciative, as well he might have been.

A confluence of interests soon led Gustav Otto to join forces with Rapp and Friz's BFW and on the 29 July, 1917 BMW, or to give it its full title the Bayerische Motoren Werke GmbH, was formed. In August 1918 the company went public and became BMW AG under the directorship of a 32 year old Viennese, the remarkable Franz Joseph Popp, whose original ambition was to have been a journalist. He was to lead the company until 1942.

BMW was born at the height of German war production, but post natal depression soon set in with Germany's surrender to the Allied forces and the harsh terms imposed in punishment upon the German people which paved the way for Hitler and the next appalling conflict.

At the time of Germany's capitulation Max Friz was working on a brand new engine. And although the Treaty of Versailles expressly forbade the Germans to build aeroplanes and the aircraft industry had accordingly abruptly ceased production, work went on in secret at the Munich complex. Friz's engine was a water-cooled inline six-cylinder design producing an astonishing 300 hp and he was determined to demonstrate just how good it was, Treaty or no Treaty. In the summer of 1919 a DFW biplane powered by BMW's new engine was flown to record heights by Franz Diemar, finally achieving 32,022ft (9,760 metres) in June. And this resulted in the Allied Commission of Control confiscating the new engine along with most of BMW's other aviation interests.

An aircraft engine manufacturer who is not allowed to go about his business in the normal way must find his workforce other things to do. BMW employed 3,500 people and Popp sadly diversified into making such unexciting things as agricultural machinery, tool boxes and office furniture, using aircraft quality materials, in order to survive. They even supplied braking systems for the railways and Friz designed a four cylinder 8 litre engine for use in heavy trucks and buses, or as a marine or stationary engine, which was not at all the sort of thing that he was used to. And it was this need for gainful occupation rather than any great enthusiasm that led to Popp making motorcycles.

BMW's first attempt to break into the motorcycle market was not a great success. The vehicle for this ambition was a lightweight with a 148cc single cylinder two-stroke proprietary engine made by Kurier. It was not sold as a BMW but was called the Flink, which would suggest that BMW themselves had little faith in the machine and the lack of sales soon justified their caution. The old Gustav Otto works was sold in 1921 in help to pay for this disaster, although BMW was subsequently able to re-purchase these facilities.

1921 also saw the introduction of a 493cc side-valve flat-twin engine, designed by Friz and designated as the M2B15, with 68 x 68mm 'square' bore and stroke dimensions which was sold to such

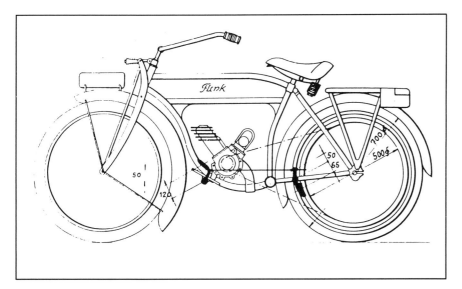

The Flink, built in 1920, was BMW's first motorcycle. The design of the single cylinder 148cc two stroke was the work of Berlin engineer Curt Hanfland.

Chief designer Max Friz, together with Martin Stolle, developed the first BMW flat twin engine, code-named M2B15, which was ready for production in 1921.

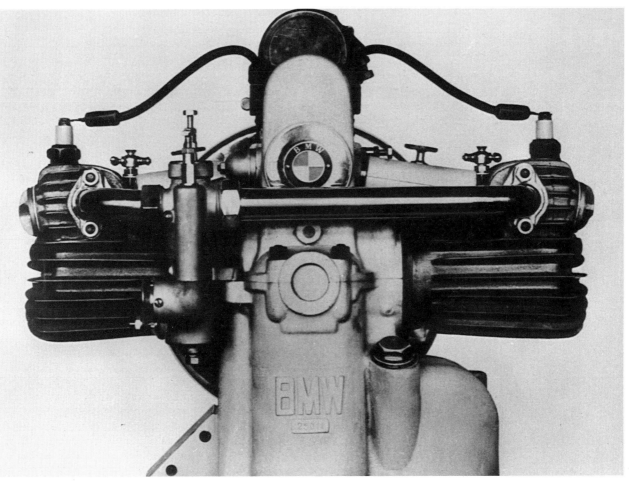

motorcycle manufacturers as SBD, SMW, Bison and Victoria, as well as several other companies. It was also used to drive the Helios, a chain-driven motorcycle built but not designed by BMW. The engine was conventionally mounted in-line with the frame and there was nothing whatsoever remarkable about it, except a general lack of any of the qualities normally associated with the products of the Munich company.

Max Friz did not care for motorcycles and he especially disliked the Helios. He felt it threatened his good reputation and, as a gifted engineer, he knew he could make a better motorcycle much as he detested them. Being unable at the time to devote his talents to designing aircraft engines, he set to work creating a machine which informed opinion would regard as worthy of the firm's distinctive badge with its stylised aircraft propeller at its centre.

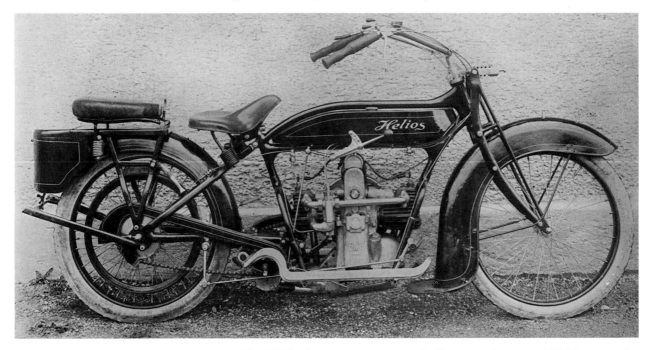

The Helios with a longitudinally-installed M2B15 engine was built by BMW in 1922. However, sales of this motorcycle with chain drive were poor.

The R32, the true ancestor of all two-wheeled BMWs, was the result. It appeared at the Paris Show in 1923 and it created a sensation. The only thing it had in common with the Helios was the capacity and configuration of the engine which was now transversely mounted in the frame. It was coupled with a car-type clutch and gearbox, had a particularly neat shaft drive and a most advanced trailing-link front fork arrangement with twin leaf springs above the mudguard. Some 3,100 R32s were built and sold over the next three years and, although it was less powerful than most of its contemporaries – its 8.5bhp would propel it at no more than 56mph (90km/h) – the springing and transmission were undoubtedly superior. Elegant and rather rakish in appearance, it was a truly modern concept in a world still dominated by machines with chain – or even belt – drive; oily, unreliable, old-fashioned engines and poor

Several other manufacturers used the M2B15 engine, including the Victoria concern.

In 1923 Max Friz designed the R32, the first BMW flat twin to have its engine mounted at right angles to the direction of travel – and featuring carden-shaft rear wheel drive.

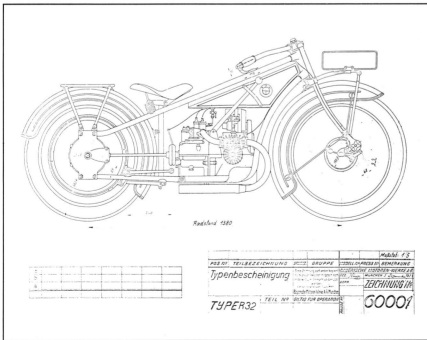

Factory technical drawing of R32.

R32 – the sensation of the 1923 Paris Motorcycle Show. Its 486cc engine gave 8.5bhp at 3300rpm.

frames. Its detractors, however, pointed out that it owed a lot to Granville Bradshaw's British ABC, which may very well be true. It would be prudent for a designer who knows nothing about motorcycles to have at least a quick look at the opposition before deciding on the layout of his own machine. But while the engine of the ABC was similar in so much as it lay across the frame, as a whole the bike was nowhere near as neat and had chain drive.

In 1924 Max Friz, having made his first and final statement on the subject, returned – no doubt with great relief – to his beloved aero engines as restrictions on their manufacture had been formally relaxed and Rudolph Schleicher took over the responsibility for motorcycles.

It was the youthful Rudolph who developed the R37. It shared the 3-speed gearbox, sturdy duplex frame and neolithic block and pulley rear wheel brake of the R32, but had an overhead valve engine which, with 16bhp at the far end of the throttle cable, raised the top speed to 71mph (115km/h). Although the R37 was much heavier – 295lbs (134kg) against the 264lbs (120kg) of the pedestrian R32 – the engine could be tuned to some effect and Franz Bieber won the German Road Racing Championship for 1924 with a 'tweaked' R37.

This potential for competition use was exploited to the full in 1925 when R37s were first across the line in over 90 road races, including a prestigious and commercially important win in the German Grand Prix. In all, 10 racing versions were constructed by the factory. The frame was gradually improved and cast alloy cylinder heads were substituted for the cast-iron items. Not only was Schleicher responsible for the development of these machines and

the preparation of Franz Bieber's racer, but he was also a good rider. He won a well deserved Gold Medal in the 1926 ISDT, which was quite a feat as the event was held in Britain whose industry and riders dominated motorcycle sport.

By 1927 BMW had made its 25,000th motorcycle. But only 175 of them were R37s; a surprisingly low number considering the marked effect that the machine had had on BMW's prestige and its immediate survival in a Germany beset by terrible financial problems consequent upon the war. For although it was the R32 that made the actual money, it was the R37's competition record that established BMW as a motorcycle manufacturer.

The R32 and the R37 had been dropped in 1926 and were followed by a succession of side-valve machines of the same capacity and very similar appearance which were gradually improved until 1928 when the range expanded to include two further models: the R62 with its 745cc side-valve engine and the sporting 733cc R63 with its overhead-valve layout and 24 brake horse power. Both bore a strong resemblance to the original R32.

Since the Armistice the workforce at BMW had steadily declined in numbers. But with motorcycles making a good profit and the aviation side expanding to build American Pratt and Whitney engines under licence, some 2,630 people were on the payroll by

Between 1923 and 1926, a total of 3100 R32s were produced at the BMW Works in Munich.

1928. Things were going well and the Board decided that the company should make the logical progression from the motorcycle business and go into car production, and they bought the Dixi plant at Eisenach in order to build cars.

Since their beginnings in the nineteenth century Dixi had been taken over twice but they were still making cars at Eisenach, no matter what was said about them! From the pre-war policy of building nicely finished horseless carriages for the upper crust, they were now reduced to building Austin 7s under licence. BMW bought out Dixi lock, stock and barrel and the Austin 7 then became BMW's first car, although it was sold under the same of Dixi until 1929 by which time BMW employed 3,860 people. This was a larger workforce than they had had in wartime.

Also in 1929 Ernst Henne began a long run of success at breaking motorcycle world speed records. Using a supercharged machine based on the 733cc engine of the firm's R63, he achieved 134.6mph (216km/h) the first time out but, while this was cheering news, Popp had other things to think about for BMW were having a hard time. They had paid an awful lot of money for the Dixi factory and, just as car production was getting under way, the economy went haywire under the strain of having to begin the annual payment of enormous sums in reparations to the Allies. And things soon went from terrible to worse when the Great Depression came along and flattened the industrialized world.

German industry was hit particularly hard. Over 17,000 companies went bankrupt but BMW were less depressed than most, although it was not the ideal time for a big investment programme in order to build cars that few people could afford to buy. In fact the car investment did pay off, not only in the future, but immediately in an unexpected way as it interested BMW in the application of pressed steel to motorcycle manufacture.

Two more 750s, the R11 and the R16 – the usual side-valve overhead-valve couple – were their first essay in this new method of constructing frames and forks and the results looked rather like cheap and nasty metal elephants. Ingenious as the 'Star' frame was, the climate was not right for selling 750s and BMW were fortunate in having aero engines that sold well in Russia and Japan while they developed a lightweight motorcycle more suited to the current market.

This was the R2, an overhead-valve single of 198cc using the pressed steel frame and forks. Not only was it cheap to buy and run, but owners did not have to pass the German driving test. The suspension of the road fund licence, or its equivalent, had the desired effect in encouraging motorcycle sales and 15,300 R2s were sold between the end of 1930 and early 1936 when it was superseded.

By January 1933 Hitler had swept to power, which pleased a lot of Germans and the majority of Europe's upper classes. BMW's first car, the 303, was on the market. In addition to the sales enjoyed by the utilitarian R2, the 398cc R4 was selling to the German army, the 733cc R16 was popular with sporting riders, BMWs were still winning lots of motorcycle races, Ernst Henne was still out there and going faster every year and 4,720 people were now employed at Eisenach and Munich. Business was picking up.

By the end of 1934 turnover was also up and stood at RM82 million. Not bad, considering that only two years earlier the company was struggling at RM19 million. By the end of 1935 it was up again to RM128 million, while the number of employees had increased to 11,113.

1935 also saw the introduction of another pair of flat-twin motorcycles: a 745cc side-valve, designated the R12 and a 733cc overhead-valve design designated the R17. They and the 305cc single cylinder R3 of 1936, which retained the ugly pressed steel forks, were the last BMWs to have the pressed steel 'Star' frame but at least the R12 and R17 had telescopic forks, another first for BMW.

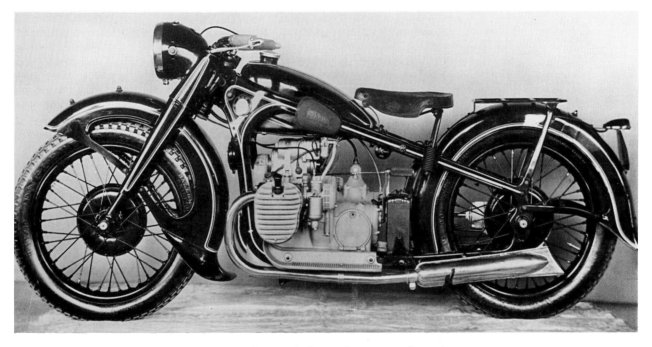

Perhaps the management had deliberately kept the pressed steel frames as it was thought that too much change at once would frighten off prospective buyers, as had so often happened in the past to other over-innovative manufacturers. Conservative as the motorcycling public was until quite recently, the new forks went down well. Not that they were actually the first teledraulic forks ever fitted to a motorcycle. But they were certainly the first with long travel and hydraulic damping ever fitted to production motorcycles. Somehow they made the pressed steel frames appear less clumsy.

In spite of BMW's pretensions to modernity, the 4-speed gearboxes of both machines were still hand-change, but the R12 was the most successful motorcycle that the company produced between the two World Wars. In all, 36,000 were sold against the 450 super-sports R17s, which says a lot about the German character. In Italy it would have been the other way around; the R17,

In 1935 the 750 R12 appeared. This was noteworthy for its use of telescopic front forks – the first employed on any mass production motorcycle.

with its 33bhp and 87mph (140km/h) would have easily out-sold the side-valve. It would be considered pretty sluggardly today, but at the time it was the quickest BMW to date. And one must remember that the octane rating of the fuel was very low; a super sports compression ratio was only 6.5 to 1 and 5,000 rpm was daring.

Nevertheless, by 1936 BMW themselves were progressing at a rate of knots. The car division, whose distinctive products were designed by Dr Fiedler, were doing well, both in terms of sales and success in competition, and were being imported into Britain by the prestigious Frazer-Nash concern. A special military equipment division was set up and the works at Eisenach began to manufacture lightweight field guns. The aircraft engine side of BMW were hard at work and the company was soon to re-occupy the Gustav Otto works which it had sold in 1921.

1936 also saw the introduction of another motorcycle: the R5 with a tubular duplex frame instead of one pressed out of steel and a 494cc engine that would turn over at 5,800 rpm. Its side-valve counterpart, the 600cc R6, appeared in 1937. And in 1938 both models were revamped, as the R51 and R61 respectively, with plunger rear suspension which was already featured on the 500cc supercharged works racers. Two more models joined the range that year: the R66, a 597cc version of the R51, and the R71 with a pressed steel frame and 745cc side-valve engine especially for sidecar work.

On 28 November 1937 Ernst Henne established a new world two wheel speed record at 173.50mph – a figure which was to remain unbeaten until 1951.

BMWs did extremely well in the ISDT for 1937 and 1938, while they had gone from strength to strength in Continental road racing. In 1937 they entered for the TT and the Ulster Grand Prix and Jock West finished in 6th place in the Isle of Man and won the Irish race. In 1938 the works team of Georg Meier, Jock West and veteran Karl Gall turned up again for the TT. But Gall fell off and hurt himself in practice, Meier retired at the starting line, and West, as BMW's sole representative, finished fifth behind three Nortons and a Velocette.

1937 BMW sporting personalities. Left to right: Kraus, Winkler (DKW), Meier, with works mechanic Hopf holding bike.

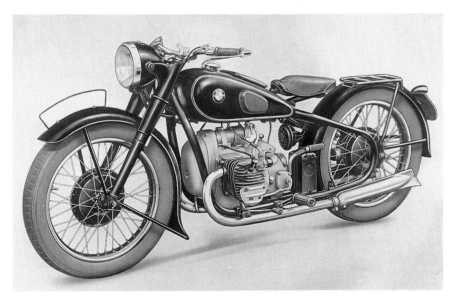

Immediate pre-war machine, the 600cc R61 – truly a luxury bike of its era.

B M W  K Series

In 1939 the trio were dispatched again, this time with bikes which looked just like the old ones but were, in fact, quite new with lots more power. Poor Gall, who had raced with BMW for years, was killed in practice but Meier's and West's machines proved so superior to the British singles, which hitherto had been unbeatable, that the Teutonic duo finished first and second with Meier declared the winner. His fastest lap was 90.75mph.

Actual supercharged works racer on which Georg Meier took victory at the 1939 Isle of Man Senior TT.

The ISDT for 1939 was held near Salzburg and was something of a non-event. The British team left halfway through and headed home as war was just about to be declared. *Korpsführer* Huhnlein was most courteous and helped in any way he could, but that was the end of international motorcycle sport for some years to come.

War is good for business for most engineering firms, especially if they happen to be experienced at making aircraft engines, guns and military vehicles. The only drawback to it is the possibility that their side might not win, for that does tend to spoil things when the fighting stops.

So it was with BMW. Even before the fighting stopped, a large proportion of the Munich works had been flattened by Allied bombing and on 11 April 1945 Hitler gave instructions that all surviving factories were to be destroyed, *immediately*. Franz Popp had finally retired in 1942 and Kurt Donath, his successor, decided to ignore this order. The Americans, when they took over, intended to dismantle what remained of BMW at Munich and ship anything of value or of interest back to the USA, but Donath also managed, somehow, to prevent this happening.

There was not much that he could do for Eisenach. During the war years the Munich factory had been fully occupied producing

The ponderous military R75. First built in 1940, it had a sidecar with differential lock, two reverse and eight forward gears. It saw widespread use by the German army during the Second World War.

aero engines and all car and motorcycle work had been transferred to the old Dixi factory which had fallen to the Red Army. They were less benevolent than the Americans – maybe because they had suffered more – and the motorcycle side of BMW was eventually sent back to Russia. After the formation of the GDR, pre-war BMW car designs reappeared as EMWs and, some years later, two-stroke Wartburg cars were built at Eisenach.

Although Donath had saved the Munich factory from oblivion, large quantities of machinery and tools were lost to the Americans. By September 1945 the workforce, now reduced to 1800, were making wood working equipment, cooking utensils, bits for bicycles or anything else that BMW found that they could sell. They even serviced military vehicles for the Americans who had given them permission to assemble 100 of the pre-war 247cc, single cylinder, R23 machines from spare parts that had managed to avoid being captured by the Russians. They also had permission to build 21,000 pedal cycles.

In 1948 the R23 was updated with a 4-speed gearbox and more power, becoming the R24, BMW's first postwar motorcycle. By the end of 1949 they had made a thousand of them and 1950 saw the introduction of a modern version known as the R25. This was basically the old R23 with plunger rear suspension. But, being a great deal neater in design, it looked more up to date and was, in fact, a much more comfortable and pleasant motorcycle.

The first postwar 500cc twin was another nice machine. This was the R51/2 which was much the same as the R51 produced before the war except for inclined downdraught carburettors. Under the direction of BMW's designer Alex von Falkenhausen, who had joined the company in 1943, BMW's policy for postwar motorcycles was to persevere with the development of the classic 'boxer' twins but to drop the side-valves from their range. And while, from 1936, some of the pre-war pushrod twins had had twin camshafts, the postwar twins from the R51/3 of 1951 had single camshaft engines.

Georg Meier had returned to racing early on with his 1939 Kompressor twin and was voted German Sportsman of the Year for 1949. But, apart from the considerable success of the Rennsport engines used in sidecar racing, BMWs have never enjoyed a prominent position in postwar motorcycle racing. Nevertheless, their

Three years after the end of hostilities BMW were able to resume motorcycle production. The 1000th R24 single rolled off the Munich production line during 1949.

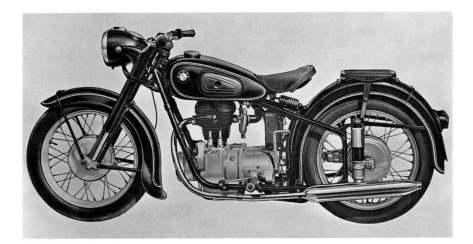

1954 247cc R25/3, very much one of the firm's mainstay models in the early post-war period – before a drastic fall in sales put the whole company at risk.

own *Wirtschaftswunder,* or 'economic miracle', was under way; the R25/3 and the R51/3 had been joined by the 590cc R67/2 and the R68 of the same capacity which was the company's first 'ton-up' twin. Up to this point BMWs had been selling well, worldwide, but suddenly the export market died. It is hard to say just why that happened, but high prices may have been responsible, at least in part. In Britain an R68 cost £440 against £273 for an Inter Norton which was almost every rider's dream machine. It was swingeing import duty that raised the price to this high level, but to the buyers that was neither here nor there.

However, things were looking good in Germany when, suddenly, in the mid 1950s it all went sour and sales fell away dramatically. And, to make things worse, the cars were not selling. BMW's response was to introduce a brand new range of extremely handsome motorcycles, civilised to a degree. These were the 247cc R26, the 494cc R50 and the 590cc R69, all with swinging arm suspension and Earles forks. This took some time to implement and it was 1955 before they all appeared, followed the next year by a gentler version of the sports R69, the touring R60.

To be less dependent on the somewhat fickle patronage of traditional enthusiasts – although they had always had a faithful following – and to diversify into a ready market for inexpensive transport where 'bubble cars' were all the rage, BMW brought out their own micro-car. Known as the Isetta, it was not their design but came from the Italian Iso concern. Originally a four-wheeler it was soon reduced to three – the rear wheels were so close together anyway that shedding one made little difference – to take advantage of insurance and road tax concessions in Britain and elsewhere. Initially the Isetta had the R25's 247cc engine – later on the R26 and 27 units were installed – and a 295cc version was introduced in December 1955. In all 74,312 250cc, and 87,416 300cc Isettas left the factory between 1955 and 1962 when production ceased.

This helped the two wheel side of BMW in that they sold a lot of engines and it was just as well they did for motorcycles were in recession. It was not only that their popularity was on the wane,

B M W _____ K Series

Wilhelm Noll gained BMW's first world sidecar championship in 1954, the start of a long period of success on three wheels.

Noll again, this time after taking the world sidecar speed record at 174.13mph on 3 October 1955.

although naturally that did not help, but BMW were making bikes that might appeal to respectable middle-aged enthusiasts, provided they were well-built, well-off and liked to change gear slowly. Beautifully engined and finished, they were ponderous and very heavy but they were built to last forever.

At 'Germany's Third Monster Motorcycle Exhibition', as *Motor Cycling* termed the 1956 Frankfurt show, BMW had nothing new to tempt the public. In fact, sales had been so poor that at the time no motorcycles whatsoever were being built at Munich. Production of Isettas had been cut back to 120 vehicles a day and stocks were building up. Had BMW not borrowed working capital from their local bank, they could well have folded there and then.

During 1957 the factory only made 5,400 motorcycles, although Isetta sales picked up a bit. 1958 was worse and by 1959 the whole of BMW – aero engines, cars and motorcycles – was on its uppers.

BMWs have been used world-wide on police duties. Here are four R60 models on escort work in Australia.

It was the shareholders, led by Dr Herbert Quandt, who saved them. Quandt had a business plan which was accepted by the creditors, but it was touch and go for Daimler Benz were keen to have the Munich factory. More capital was raised, not only from the banks who might have lost a lot of money if BMW went under, but also from the sale of the aero engine business to MAN Turbo GmbH. Hermann Richter-Brohm, the Managing Director, had to go and his post was taken by Karl-Heinz Sonne who sanctioned the improvements to the motorcycles and a whole new range of cars.

The specially constructed 600cc supercharged road-going BMW racer presented to Walter Zeller in 1958 following his retirement from racing.

It was the first new car, a 4-door 1500 launched at the Frankfurt Show in 1961, that transformed the fortunes of the company and was the cornerstone of their success. Not entirely on its merits, but with aggressive marketing techniques that had hitherto been anathema to BMW. In the 1960s the car division went from strength to strength, while the motorcycles languished. The management considered dropping motorcycles altogether, but were loath to do so. Quite why it is hard to say. Maybe from a feeling that tradition was important, that it would be sad to see the disappearance of a famous marque with a reputation for integrity and quality unrivalled by any other manufacturer. Or maybe out of loyalty to the customers who had been loyal to BMWs. Whatever prompted them it was not profit, unless they had a crystal ball.

Ironically, throughout the 1960s BMWs dominated sidecar racing, but little of the sporting spirit was manifested in the road machines in spite of the improvements mentioned. Two so-called sports machines, the R50S and the R69S, were added to the range, the 42 bhp – 110mph R69S being the flagship. *Motor Cycle* described it as . . . "A luxury roadster with superb high speed performance, docile traffic manners, magnificent steering, road holding and brakes." In short, a lovely motorcycle but not one to set prospective buyers emptying their piggy banks. Especially as the

United Kingdom price was £530; roughly twice that of a high performance British vertical twin.

In spite of this apparent lack of interest on the part of management, things were stirring on the motorcycle front. In April 1965 the *Motor Cycle* carried details of a new range of 'boxer' twins then being developed at the Munich works. Editor Harry Louis rode a prototype around Bavaria for several days and was most impressed. Whereas the R69S weighed 445lbs – (202kg), the bike that Louis rode was 65lbs (29.5kg) lighter. It was equipped with 'teles', it had a shallow seat, narrow handlebars and mudguards, it was fast and handled beautifully. The first inkling of what was on the way had come in 1964 when the ISDT machines appeared with telescopic forks, light duplex frames and 54bhp engines.

British rider George Catlin being pushed into life on the MLG R69S which broke the 24 hour world record at Montlhery, France on 3 March 1961, averaging 109.36mph.

During this period the motorcycle side of BMW was moved to Spandau, as the all-important car production was very short of space at Munich. An interim range for the American market was produced in 1968 to cater for a Stateside craze for 'off-road' riding. They had new gearboxes, telescopic forks and high rise bars to distinguish them from the standard Earles fork range and they were designated the R50US, the R60US, and the R69US. The real 'new look' range was the responsibility of Hans-Gunther von der Marwitz – BMW went in for noblemen when appointing their designers – who had joined the company in 1964 and they appeared, by luck or perfect timing, later in 1969. Just in time to take advantage of the upsurge of interest in motorcycling sparked off by the Japanese and the invention of the Superbike.

There were three new machines. A 500, a 600 and a 750 which was intended as a Superbike. The 250 had been dumped back in 1967. The R50/5, the R60/5 and the R75/5 all had flat twin engines which were very much the same. The old roller bearing big-ends with their 50,000 mile life span had been discarded. The new engines shared the same forged cranks and the same enormous conrods – with plain big-end bushes – which originated from a four wheeled BMW. The only differences between the engines were the variations in the carburation, crankshaft balancing arrangements and the bore diameters. These were 67, 73.5 and 82mm respectively, giving capacities of 498, 599 and 746cc, while the cylinders were of light alloy with cast iron pressed-in liners and aluminium heads. The new, much lighter, frames were made up of two loops of oval tubing with the rear section bolted on and telescopic forks, developed from the ISDT models, graced the front of the machines.

1969 saw the arrival of the Stroke 5 series, including the R75/5 (pictured). Also a new home for BMW motorcycles at Spandau, West Berlin.

The new /5 Series bikes were not perfect, but they were a great deal better from a performance point of view, than what had gone before. More importantly, they were also a great deal better than most of their competitors. And while the handling might not be quite as good as that of the better British and Italian machines, they were a lot more comfortable.

The slight handling deficiencies of the early /5 Series were attributable to the shortish wheelbase and were exacerbated by worn tyres – all BMWs are sensitive to tyre wear and especially sensitive to tyres not recommended by the factory. This was corrected in the later models by lengthening the swinging arm by 2 inches (50mm) which increased the wheelbase and improved stability at speed. But there are those who say that this was done to make room for a larger battery.

The first /5s had been acceptable to purists. God had sensibly decreed that all BMWs should be a glossy black and some eyebrows had been raised at the silver tanks and mudguards which were offered as an option. But the Auto Union and Mercedes Grand Prix cars had lent respectability to silver. In 1972 a further heresy crept in when smaller, flatter, petrol tanks *with chrome plated side panels* were offered and the gaps between the main frame and the

Six times in a row – between 1967 and 1974 – Klaus Enders won the Manufacturers' World Sidecar championship for BMW. 1/23

sub-frame were filled by metal panels each side. That was bad enough, but the /6 range was blasphemy. They appeared in gaudy shades of mustard, blue and green as well as black and silver and they shocked the faithful, very deeply.

The /6s were the first of the truly modern 'boxer' twins. They were launched at the Paris Show in October 1973 – the R32 had been launched in Paris fifty years before – and they hoisted BMW to the top of the Superbike league with two brand new 900cc models: the R90/6 and the R90S. The other models in the range were the R60/6 and the R75/6. The 500cc model had been dropped after half a century. All four engines shared the same 70.6mm stroke, the two largest achieving their 898cc capacity with 90mm bores. For the first time in their history BMW employed a stylist, Hans Muth, from the Ford Motor Company. He designed the seat and fairing and introduced the striking air-brush finish of the R90S.

Left: **1971 Isle of Man TT. Hans-Otto Butenuth took fourth place on a R75/5 in the Production event, then followed it up in 1973 with a ninth.**

Launched at the Paris Show fifty years after the R32, in October 1973, the R90S sportster featured Hans Muth–styled bikini fairing.

There were other fundamental changes. Single hydraulic disc brakes on the front wheels came as standard on the R75/6 and the R90/6 while the R90S, the flagship, had twin discs on the front and the R60/6 had drum brakes all round. The rear suspension could be adjusted to three positions and all four bikes had 5-speed gearboxes. The early version of this gearbox gave some trouble and had to be recalled. The crankcases were strengthened to cope with the power increases and there were new silencers, headlamps, instrument consoles, control levers and plastic side panels.

Around this time there was a plan that BMW and Puch, the Austrian bicycle and motorcycle manufacturers, should join forces to produce a new range of 250 and 350cc overhead camshaft parallel twins. Unlike BMW, Puch had spare capacity and for this reason it was intended that the new machines should be made at Graz, in Austria, at a projected rate of 25,000 a year and marketed as BMW-Puchs. BMW were short of labour at the Spandau plant and it was hinted that Puch might help them out by producing parts for the flat twins. Both these projects fizzled out, although a few prototype BMW-Puchs were made.

For 1975 there were only minor changes. The kickstarters were finally removed to make room for a better gear change mechanism, the starter motors were uprated and the R90S had perforated discs which howled, although that was unintentional, the perforations beng intended to improve wet weather braking.

The Cologne Show of '76 saw the launching of the /7 Series and, more significantly, BMW's last major effort to keep the 'boxer' engine in the forefront of the power race which was hotting up. Their contender was the 980cc engine and, although won Marwitz had intimated that the 90mm bores of the 890cc engine had left the liners a bit thin, he managed to increase the bore to 94mm. This, with a compression ratio of 9.5 to 1 and larger exhaust and inlet tracts, actually gave 2bhp less than the engine that it superseded – they soon found another 5bhp – but massively improved the torque over a wide power band.

Not only was the engine most impressive, but it appeared in a dramatic setting in the fully streamlined R100RS. Other manufacturers had already offered comprehensive fairings, but this was the world's first successful fully faired production motorcycle. And BMW had gone to considerable expense to ensure it was successful, having hired Pininfarina's wind tunnel at £2,500 a day. The R100RS cost £2,899 in the UK, £900 more than its most expensive shaft drive rival, the Le Mans Moto Guzzi. But *Motor Cycle Mechanics'* Bob Goddard wrote that ". . . in all the major requirements of a very serious motorcycle for very serious (and wealthy) enthusiasts, the R100RS is outstanding." BMW had upstaged the Japanese.

The R60/7, the R75/7 and the R100/7 were the supporting cast and, with the 'star', they held the fort for BMW until 1977 when production peaked at 31,231 units. After that it was downhill all the way, if only gradually at first. Even the seductive shape of the R100RS could not for long disguise the fact that the 'boxer' engine had reached the limit of development and had had its day in so far as it was failing to attract enough new buyers.

Having said that, one of the nicest of all 'boxers' had not yet appeared. This was the 797cc R80/7 which *Motorcycle International* have just elevated to the status of a Practical Classic. It replaced the R75/7 in 1978 in a range that featured nineteen improvements of a minor nature. The R100/7 gained another, much needed, disc at the front wheel, the R100RS got a single disc for its rear wheel while the others soldiered on with drum brakes at the rear.

1979 saw a successful return to the rigours of the ISDT by BMW with this 55bhp 750cc class flat twin.

Spandau production line in the late 1970s.

B M W

Fuel tanks still lined by hand.

Far right: **1980** also saw the introduction of the highly rated R80 G/S trail bike.

The Cologne Show in September 1980 saw the supercharged Futuro prototype displayed – it never entered production.

BMW won the motorcycle category of the Paris-Dakar Rally no less than four times – 1981, 1983, 1984 and 1985. Here is the '85 version of the 'King of the Desert' bike.

Autumn of that year saw BMW making a real effort to gain a profitable foothold in the medium weight market. An effort that failed miserably as the 473cc R45 was easily the most lifeless motorcycle that the company had made for years while the 649cc R65, which replaced the ageing R60, was little better. The 45 and 65 were exactly the same size and weight. Physically they were shorter than the others in the range and they were also lower as they had smaller wheels – 18in instead of 19in – in cast light alloy.

Right: Touring first class – by R100RT in the early 1980s. By now the flat twin concept was beginning to feel its age.

The R100RS was eventually joined by the fully faired touring version of the 980cc twins designated the R100RT. Cast alloy wheels came in as standard. And BMWs were a great hit with the British police, but in retreat elsewhere. The last BMW flat twin of any great significance was the 797cc R80GS trail bike. It was not only a fine motorcycle in itself – Graham Sanderson of *Motor Cycle Weekly* described it as 'BMW's best roadster' – but it influenced a range of BMWs as yet unborn. Change was needed, very badly. And change was on the way.

B M W

R80S/T. Developed from the G/S, it was a fine motorcycle but was overshadowed by the appearance of the first K-Series machines, the K100 four, and was soon dropped.

1923 – 83 – sixty years of the BMW flat twin. But also, and more importantly as regards this book, the year in which the K-Series was first available.

2

Conception and Evolution

By the late 1970s the motorcycle division of BMW was in big trouble. Its motorcycle sales were holding up in Britain but nowhere else. It had slumped to 7th spot in the home market and, worse still, into 11th place behind Husqvarna in the USA where it had 7,000 bikes unsold. Rudolph von der Schulenberg had resigned as chairman and the chief engineer and sales director had both gone, beneath a cloud, to other, unspecified, employment in the factory. From 1 January, 1979 the new men at the handlebars were Dr Wolfgang Aurich and Dr Karl H Gerlinger under the chairmanship of Dr Eberhardt C Sarfert. All three were expert motorcyclists in their middle forties and it was their urgent task to choose the road the company should take.

One choice was obvious enough. BMW could give up bikes and concentrate on cars where there was much less effective opposition from the Japanese, but its tribulations could not be blamed, entirely, on the Japanese. The low sales ratings in the States stemmed, at least to some degree, from the wish to set up an American subsidiary to sell its own machines and Butler & Smith of New York City, who had been the BMW concessionaires for years, were accordingly less enthusiastic than they might otherwise have been and motorcycle sales had fallen off dramatically.

However, BMW's own products were the major problem that Dr Sarfert had to face. Like Butler & Smith, the 'boxer' twins had been around for years and on the motorcycle scene they had begun to look like sensible and sober matrons at an art school dance attended by a crowd of gorgeous, nubile, Orientals. Not unnaturally, the sober matrons were neglected and the realisation that the enchanting Japanese were mostly superficial trollops had yet to dawn upon a world conditioned to expect integrity in motorcycle engineering. There had been bad bikes before, many of them British, but built-in obsolescence was an unexpected factor.

To make things worse the motorcycle press, who showed little interest in unreliability, shattering spares prices or the unavailability of spares for those who could afford them, praised the competition to the skies. Unfortunately, some of the technically advanced and glamorous machines from Suzuki, Honda, Yamaha and Kawasaki, were very good indeed. They handled well, they went extremely rapidly – bikes that looked much like them were winning Grand Prix races – and on the face of it they were not expensive. They made BMW's old fashioned virtue of longevity with the simplicity of only 5-speeds in the gearbox, however adequate, and two fairly low-tech cylinders sticking out each side, just as they had for fifty years, look pretty dull. The buyers stayed away in droves. And even such traditional BMW enthusiasts as the motorcycling bourgeoisie defected to the Japanese. Ironically, the company was also having trouble with quality control and the few buyers that existed were finding fault with parts supplied by foreign manufacturers. The time had obviously come for change.

The displaced management had seen this situation coming, but not soon enough. They had hoped that such environmental pressures as low speed limits and the rising cost of oil would end the escalating horsepower race and emasculate the opposition. And if logic were a major factor in the battle to sell motorcycles, their directive that the firm should soldier bravely on with the outmoded 'boxer' twins would have paid off handsomely.

When it did not somebody made another wrong decision and commissioned a design team, who knew very little about motorcycles, to build a futuristic bike. Vorsprung durch Technik is all very well, but this ill-conceived device was technically several jumps behind the Japanese and used a turbo-charged flat-twin engine and the standard 5-speed gearbox. These were mounted in a part tubular, part monocoque chassis wrapped in a low low fairing that would have looked at home in Gotham City. Ergonomically disastrous, the low position caused the rider great discomfort but the handling in cross-winds, exacerbated by the slab-sided tail and disc front wheel, might have helped him to forget his pain although it would certainly have occasioned mental anguish. BMW called it the Futuro and exhibited the prototype at the Cologne show in 1980 but, as much as Batman would have loved it, it was not a success and did not feature in their future plans.

For a company that had been extremely cautious about innovation almost since the day of the decision to use the teledraulic fork, the Futuro was strangely out of character and most probably reflected the bewilderment of management. Dr Sarfert was made of sterner stuff. Having made his mind up that BMW should stay and fight, he shrugged off the Futuro, sanctioned a new trail bike that turned out to be a very pleasant motorcycle to cash in on the craze for off-road bikes – most of which stayed firmly on the tarmac – and spurred the R&D department on to further efforts.

Under the old management, designer Josef Fritzenwenger had been beavering away since 1975, trying to find a viable and acceptable alternative to the 'boxer' twins, but brute force had never much appealed to R&D at Spandau, although in the 1970s great dollops of unnecessary power was apparently the feature that sold large quantities of motorcycles. "It ain't whatcha do, it's the way thatcha do it" could well have been their motto and this is still the case. It might even sound more dignified in German. They had been most reluctant to stretch the 600cc engine to 746cc and even more unhappy when falling sales dictate that they must increase capacity to 980cc in the search for yet more brake horse power in a vain attempt to keep up with the 'threes' and 'fours' and 'sixes' that kept arriving from Japan. Under protest, they eventually experimented with an even bigger version of the twin with water cooling but, having experienced its low speed shakes which would have appalled a hardened tractor driver, everyone agreed that it was not a pleasant engine.

The logical extension of the flat-twin engine would have been a liquid cooled flat four – according to the press they had built one years before, but nothing was ever seen of it. It would have been a most attractive bike and one in keeping with the firm's tradition, but whether or not they seriously considered it we probably shall never know. And if they had, Honda's introduction of the flat four, water-cooled Gold Wing would have stifled it at birth. BMW had no intention of fighting on a battleground chosen by the competition.

The new management strongly disapproved, and said so, of the short-sighted route chosen by the Japanese towards their intended domination of the world's motorcycle market. A rapid succession of highly complex, under-developed and economically irreparable machines was not their style and would have harmful repercussions on the sales of motorcycles. Over-production and consequent price-cutting would drive many dealers out of business and dilute the quality of the services available to customers, while the blatant advertising of quite excessive speed and power would attract repressive legislation.

BMW was seeking an up-to-date successor to the 'boxer' twins in the same civilised tradition. The new range would, of necessity, be based upon a model that would remain recognisably the same into the 1990s and beyond thus amortizing the huge cost of thoroughly developing the new machines which would comply with current and foreseeable legislation for some years to come.

The management were optimistic for the long-term prospects, predicting an increase in leisure time and an expanding leisure market. In their own words: "There will be an increased desire to fill this free space with more individual activities. The search for more adventure and experience in life will expand the leisure and hobby market of the future in many and various ways (polls predicting a doubling by 1990). The trend towards sophisticated, high-quality leisure time equipment will increase substantially. In spite of the much quoted change in attitudes to and public discussion about the motorcycle, it will have its place in this growing segment of the leisure market for it is a fascinating spare-time machine and permits unconventional self-realization."

Without wishing to be in any way political, all that is rather reminiscent of the attitudes of intellectuals of the early 1900s when predicting the emancipation of mankind through automation. Certainly the current trend is towards more leisure via unemployment but, if BMW can sell enough machines to the upward mobility and gentry of the world's stock markets to make it worth their while, they may be right. They may even profit from the inevitable left-wing backlash by selling BMWs to commissars with lots of leisure time.

However, their search for the sporting status symbol of the 1990s was further complicated by the need to retain their 'distinctive' image, which meant that vertical twins, V twins of all kinds, square fours, transverse multis, two-strokes and chain drive were all unthinkable, which narrowed down the choice a bit.

It was the experiments that Josef Fritzenwenger carried out with a water-cooled, four cylinder engine from a Peugeot car that led him to the concept of the CDS, or Compact Drive System as BMW was soon to call it. The primary attraction of the 1 litre aluminium engine was its low weight and the small staff of the modest motorcycle R&D department soon contrived a chassis to house this automotive power-plant. It was intended for transverse and inclined installation in the Peugeot 104 and it soon struck Fritzenwenger that if he took its natural inclination one stage further and laid the engine flat, but with its crankshaft in line with the frame, it could be just what he was looking for – a striking combination of practicality and exclusivity.

The configuration had several great advantages; a low centre of gravity, mechanical accessibility and innate suitability for the obligatory shaft drive. The management, as Fritzenwenger had imagined, were thrilled with the idea. For them the clincher was the exclusivity, especially as such an engine layout was even more unusual than the 'boxer' twin which had its look-a-likes and even had a predecessor in the ABC flat-twin of 1921. No-one in the motorcycle business made a longitudinal and horizontal in-line four or, so far as they knew, had ever made an engine like it.

Nevertheless, they were still cautious. Since 1973 bike production at the Spandau factory had run at 10% of the Munich factory's car production and, as the company's cars cost on average four times as much as 'boxer' twins, it followed that the motorcycle division's R&D department were strictly on a budget and could not afford to 'get it wrong'.

In 1977 Fritzenwenger got the go-ahead to develop his new engine. The project was some distance down a fairly lengthy cul-de-sac due to the management being understandably seduced by the current popularity of "monster" motorcycles. It was eventually decided to make two versions of the engine: an 800 to 1000cc three, designated the K3, and 1300cc four, designated the K4, both closely based upon the car division's engines. The cylinder heads were on the right hand side of both machines, the same side as the drive shaft, which made it very hard to find a satisfactory place on which to mount the silencer. The valve gear was not happy at high speed and the only tangible achievement after eighteen months or so was the certain knowledge that motorcycles with large engines are wide, long, very heavy and appeal only to a market restricted to strong men with abnormally long arms.

With no clear directives from above, R&D were floundering when Dr Sarfert swept to power. Whatever else the doctor ordered, it would not be a surrogate Münch Mammoth and Fritzenwenger paused for breath while the new management took stock. It was their opinion that enormous motorcycles would shortly be extinct, which left them with the problem of finding a new range in BMW's own image. And in addition to their own requirements, there were other points to be considered before they came to a conclusion. Technical trends, long term market developments, stricter emission and noise

In the late 1970s tests were undertaken with various three and four cylinder layouts. Shown here is the K3, a prototype with a 1000cc three cylinder engine, year 1977.

With a view to projecting the marque's civilised image, BMW undertook comprehensive silencer testing, including even double-barreled types.

controls, and the sacred relationship between cost and selling price had to be examined; without a crystal-ball this sort of thing takes time.

The accountants were quite keen to have a transverse, in-line, chain-drive four on the grounds that it was cheap, but this soulless and short-sighted policy, which would have proved disastrous, was sensibly rejected. Several other engine layouts were investigated but, having looked at all the possibilities, the attractions of the Compact Drive system, properly developed, were even more apparent.

Designer Josef Fritzenwenger (right) discusses cylinder head detail with another member of the development team.

Measuring technique with a prototype.

Properly developed was, of course, the key. And that would not be possible with Fritzenwenger's small team of empiricists that was currently engaged on R&D. On 20 February, 1979, only seven weeks after the new management had taken over, the Board of BMW AG sanctioned their decision to commit the future of the two wheel division of the company to two versions of the innovative CDS and the R&D department dramatically and suddenly expanded to a full complement of 240 dedicated souls.

At 35, Stefan Pachernegg was given overall responsibility for developing the new machines, a heavy burden which may have caused his untimely death. At 36, Josef Fritzenwenger was Design Engineer; Gunther Schier, 49, was Head of Running Gear Development; Martin Probst, at 45, was Head of Engine Development; Richard Heydenreich, 54, was Head of Vehicle Development and, at 42, Klaus-Volker Gevert became the Head of the Design Department.

The overworked Pachernegg was also a member of Dr Sarfert's

management and he did not have an easy task. The new machines would have to have an individual life expectancy exceeding that of the flat-twins; and that alone was a tall order as well looked-after twins often reached a ripe old age. And the Compact Drive System, which was the heart of the new range, had to be so well designed that it would still be technically acceptable in twenty, or more, years ahead. BMW is fundamentally opposed to change unless it is absolutely necessary. In 1979 the 'boxer' twins had been around for almost sixty years. In addition to these modest aims, the new bikes would have to be fast without being too fast; flexible with bags of mid-range torque; have to steer and handle beautifully and yet have comfortably soft suspension; be ultra-modern in appearance and yet be practical and saleable; and also be quiet, light, manoeuvrable, economical and basically fairly simple so as to be easy to maintain and repair. At the same time they would be expected to be all things to all men – 'supersports road-burner', long distance tourer and most things in between and, as if that were not enough, they would have to subtly conform to the popular image of what a BMW should be, which involved blending flair and dash with dignity.

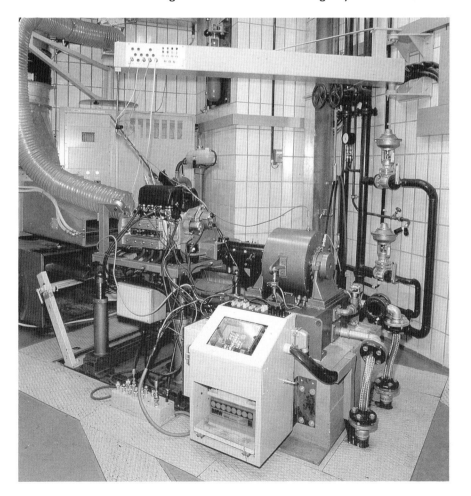

Pre-production engine on the test bench.

Development: Top, a cardan shaft with mechanical shock absorber; below, the standard design with rubber shock absorbers.

Head of design Klaus-Volker Gevert (standing) watches a colleague preparing a design sketch.

Below: BMW motorcycle design chief Klaus-Volker Gevert (front) and other members of the team discussing one of the innumerable designs. Note feet forward creation on wall – and another interesting design to its right.

Below right: Test department – prototypes of the definitive K100 series under construction.

The engine, gearbox and drive shaft units gave Martin Probst a task well suited to his temperament. It was a logical extension of his past work since he, with Paul Rosche, had been responsible for making the BMW four cylinder car engine the most successful Formula 2 power unit of all time. The development of a compact high-performance power pack for a thoroughly modern motorcycle was just 'up his Strasse' and an appropriate and challenging way to continue his career. It was decided that 90bhp was the right amount of power to aim for from what was now to become a four of 987cc while the three with a capacity of 740cc would be expected to produce 75bhp, both coupled with a good power curve which left considerable scope for output to be uprated at a later date if that should prove to be desirable, or necessary.

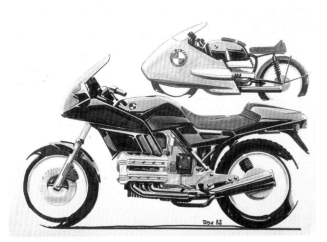

Above left: **Old and new: An early design study of the K100RS in the foreground with a fully-streamlined 500RS racing machine of the 1950s.**

Above: **Styling model for standard K100 using tailor-made cubing design process.**

Pre-production K100 undergoing road testing.

Work on the two-tier range began at Spandau in the May of 1979. But as there is little information to be had regarding the thought processes involved in the evolution of the K100, we shall scan its technicalities in another chapter and confine ourselves here to problems that distracted the design team. These, by all accounts, were few if not far between.

Mock-up of CDS (Compact Drive System), a vital ingredient of the K-Series concept.

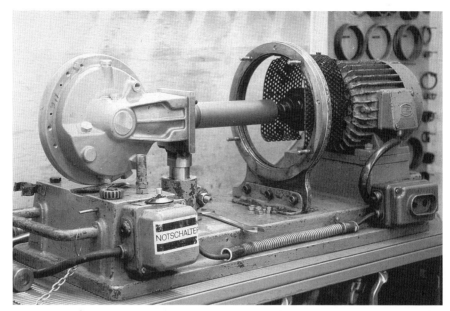

Endurance testing a cardan shaft with vibration damper and rear wheel drive.

Monolever in three variations: Left, a tubular steel design; at its side two development stages in cast light alloy.

Three views of early three-cylinder model drawings produced in 1981 for the forthcoming K75 series.

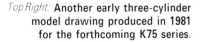

Top Right: Another early three-cylinder model drawing produced in 1981 for the forthcoming K75 series.

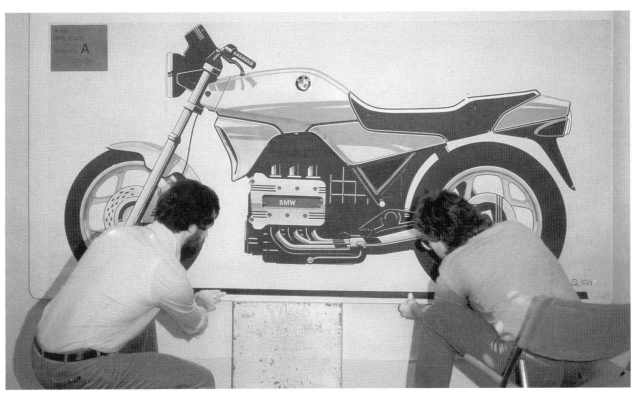

The troubles that have been confessed centred upon reducing loud, intrusive noises from the gears coupling the crankshaft and the secondary engine shaft that drives the clutch. The original design employed two gearwheels of exactly the same size – a ratio of 1 to 1 – no matter how these gears were cut or whatever quantity of oil was directed over them, they still made a disturbing meshing sound. The eventual solution was to use two gears upon the secondary shaft, one much wider than the other, but adding up to the same width as the original gear, the two halves held a 'gnat's whisker' apart and half a tooth out of alignment by a circlip-like spring between the two.

Above left: Initially, vibrations in the three-cylinder engine gave engineers a headache. The drive damper used was not suitable – and the clutch plate used (see photo) was subject to failure.
Above: The smaller and lighter clutch (based on the R80 flat twin type), shown with a so-called swash-plate, solved the earlier problems.

An early prototype K75S with hand covers on the fairing during wind tunnel testing, circa early 1983.

The final prototype which appeared too similar to the K100RS and was discarded.

Even the choice of colours was an important task in the BMW schedule.

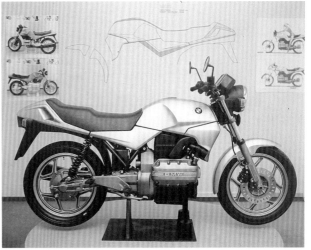

The K75C was originally what BMW described as a 'classic' – without any kind of fairing. These two views above show what it would have looked like had it not been discarded before the launch. However a very similar style was adopted in 1986 for the unfaired K75. Note ugly K100 silencer.

As well as countless miles out on the road, BMW also used a robot system which, with steel arms and pneumatic muscles, was able to operate the throttle and clutch, change gears and apply the brakes 24 hours a day – something a human test rider found it difficult enough to do during an eight hour working day.

When the helical gear on the crankshaft is in mesh with the two driven gears, the sprung half is forced into alignment but takes up any backlash which stops the irritating noise.

In view of all the trouble that they went to in order to hush-up these gears, it would have seemed more logical to use a toothed plastic or rubber belt to drive the camshafts, but this would have meant a separate, oil free compartment for the belt to run in. For this reason a chain was chosen, its inherent thrashings kept in moderately silent check by a rubber faced chain tensioner as well as

Tape recorders were used during testing to measure various running conditions, including brake pressure, pedal forces and wheel speed as well as temperature of the brake drums, discs and fluid.

The data stored on tape was then transferred to a plotter following the tests themselves. The figures measured were shown in lines of various colours.

the usual automatic chain adjuster and plastic faced guides behind both camshaft sprockets.

It is hard to imagine that a totally new engine could be developed with so little strain. But, if the official version is to be believed, once Probst had applied himself to 'lateral thinking' and turned the engine round so that the cylinder head was on the left instead of on the right as in the K3 and the K4 prototypes, it was more or less plain sailing. The only exception was the inconvenience of having to subdue the gear noise which did take the engine team some time.

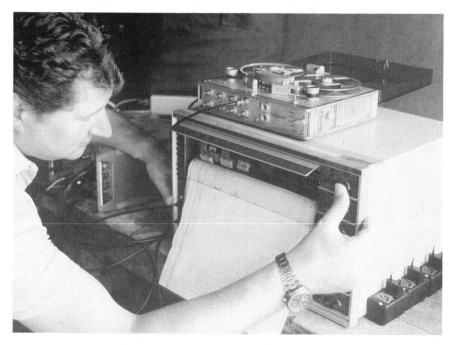

Gunther Schier, assisted by Klaus Erdmann, had the job of 'adding lightness' to the running gear, or rolling chassis, as the Compact Drive System was expected to weigh 44lbs (20kg) more than the 'boxer' engine and transmission and BMW was keen to keep the all-up weight of the new bikes roughly at the level of the old R-Series twins. As all roadworthy motorcycles for a given purpose require the same equipment, in affordable materials, this just was not possible, but the eventual 474lbs (215kg) of the basic K100 was quite acceptable and astonishingly light by current standards.

Some weight saving was achieved because the Compact Drive System acted as a frame, the latter item being a lightweight structure on which to hang the forks and support the seat and tank. More weight was saved by using simple teledraulic forks with no fashionable adjustment for the springs and shock absorbers, variable air support, or a lot of gaudy 'stickers' to advertise their presence. It was Gunther Schier's opinion that it was the manufacturer's and not the rider's job to tune the bike correctly and the old engineering adage that 'If something can go wrong, it will' was probably behind

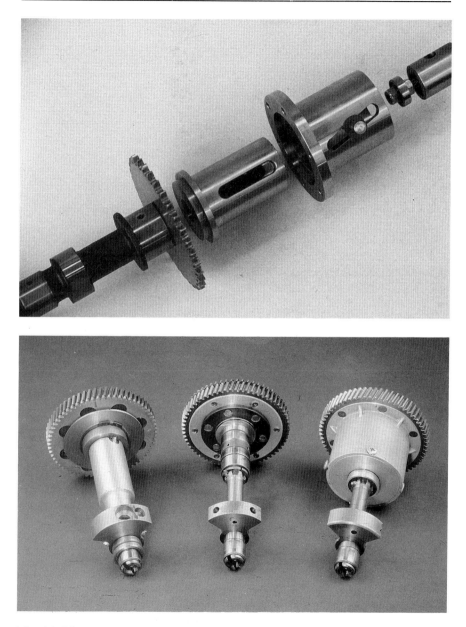

In developing the new water-cooled engines BMW's engineers used adjustable camshafts in the dynamometer tests to determine optimum valve timing. Tests proved the 3-cylinder was able to run with the same valve timing as the larger engine, despite its higher specific output.

The 3-cylinder engine required counterweights on the drive shaft to balance the free mass momentum. The shaft therefore also served as an equalizing force. Development was not an easy task, the first experiments with shafts incorporating a drive damper failing to provide the necessary success. Compare these with the production solution in the K75 chapter.

Above: Many alternatives were considered in the design of the water pump gears. Not only the design, but also the material used. Grey-cast iron, metal plate and plastic were all tried.

his thinking. Adjustable suspension can be very dangerous if set up badly and related accidents are bound to happen. Nor were Schier and Erdmann much impressed by the contemporary crop of anti-dive systems to counter fork reaction under heavy braking. 'The best thing you can do with them,' Stefan Pachernegg said crisply, 'is to leave them out.'

Initially the whole team concentrated on K589 as the 4 cylinder project was designated at the factory, as it was intended to be launched in four years' time as the first of the new range. But even at this early stage some basic information was collected for the 3

The K-Series development team
Stefan Pachernegg.
Right: Josef Fritzenwenger.
Far right: Gunter Schier.

Right: The Management of BMW Motorrad GmbH at the time of the K100 launch in Autumn 1983. Left to right: the late Stefan Pachernegg (development), Hans Glas (production), Karl Gerlinger (sales and distribution) and Dr Eberhardt Sarfert (chairman and member of the Board of BMW AG).

cylinder project, known as K569, since the individual cylinders were conceived and planned with largely the same features. And the auxiliary components were also to be much the same, if not actually identical. Probst and his colleagues were determined from the beginning to balance out the free first-order mass forces – more elegantly termed the rocking couple – of the three by employing a balancer shaft, or a wobble knocking shaft; an old fashioned name for the same thing.

Work on the three intensified as soon as the four was going strongly. One of the first priorities was to obtain a bit more power without encroaching on the fundamental characteristics of a very pleasant engine by using bigger valves and 'hotter' valve timings, which would have increased engine speed and spoilt the torque curve at low revs.

With this in mind, the engineers began studying the potential of K589's combustion chambers and obtained significant improvements by changing the profile of the cylinder head to that of a stump cone and matching it with a convex crown piston with pockets for the valves. To increase engine power still more, the team attempted to improve the 'breathing' and eventually succeeded by using shorter inlet manifolds and by modifying the exhaust system to incorporate three shorter pipes housed inside one larger pipe at the front of the three-cornered silencer.

When the K569 3-cylinder engine was first run on the dynamometer in September 1982, a problem that had already arisen when the earlier K3 type three was tested reared its destructive head once more. In the cause of economy through uniformity, Martin Probst had tried to use a K100 drive shaft, but with balance weights attached, and it was soon discovered that they caused damage to the

The K-series development team
Klaus-Volker Gevert.
Far left: Richard Heydenreich.
Left: Martin Probst.

B M W

The first stage of the K-Series evolution – K100, K100RT and K100RS, with one of the company's four wheel prestige products in the background for once.

integrated rubber damper unit on the shaft. The increased firing gaps imposed greater loads at longer intervals and the damper was totally destroyed, but this was eventually overcome by specifying a larger section, un-damped shaft.

There were more vibration problems when the K100's hefty, rigidly connected clutch was applied to the new three, but these were solved, after a lengthy struggle, by fitting an R80 clutch, much modified to cope with different load conditions, which also acted as a damper. The engine development group were preoccupied with this unexpected setback until the summer of 1983 and the first customers were running-in their K100s when the first K75 engines were running on the dynamometer for 300-hour endurance tests.

Road testing began in the winter of 1983 with the engines fitted into modified K100 chassis, while Gunther Schier's department were pondering the possibilities of a new frame for the three. In the end the standard frame was used, but with the front supports set back at a greater angle towards the rear.

BMW was anxious that the K75-Series should be unique motorcycles in their own right and not to be considered as poor relations of the K100. Long before the road test stage was reached, Klaus-Volker Gevert and his department had completed detailed drawings for the K75S, which was to be the 'flagship' of the threes with its own distinctive streamlined fairing. In order to emphasise the bike's own clear identity, it was agreed at the beginning that the fairing would not follow the example set by the shape developed for the K100RS model and intended to give the rider almost complete protection from the wind, but should underline the K75's lower weight and better handling. Like the 'RS' fairing, it was evolved for optimum efficiency in BMW's own wind tunnel and achieved its stated aims – at the cost of some discomfort for the taller rider – while at the same time discouraging any tendency to lift at speed.

When the first pre-production versions of the K75 were built at the Spandau factory during March 1985, Pachernegg was able to present a positive report: "With the exception of the drive train we had fewer unexpected problems than with the K100. Still, we have to consider that the K75 was developed two years later and therefore benefited from all the good and bad experience we had already gained with the K100. All we had to do, therefore, was to introduce the necessary improvements for the K75."

The cost of developing the K75 was just half of that incurred for the gestation of the K100. The building-brick system as BMW have termed it (rather aptly as the motorcycle press named the K100 'The Flying Brick') had paid off handsomely.

3

K 100

The first fruits of these exhaustive, costly and long-rumoured labours was introduced to an eagerly waiting public in October 1983. And if there was a moment of stunned silence before the tumult of acclaim and criticism, it must have been extremely brief. That the unfaired K100, soon to be followed by suitably 'clothed' sports and touring versions of the same machine, could create such a furore in a world already satiated by two-wheelers of staggering performance and sensational appearance says a great deal for the rightness of Josef Fritzenwenger's concept of a modern motorcycle. Particularly one intended as a practicable means of transport with a considerable life span, sensibly aloof from the philosophy of disposable projectiles of paranormal power and speed and very limited utility, aimed at an illusory mass market with an endless appetite for change.

At the time the motorcycle press made much of the courage shown by BMW in introducing a luxurious machine at what was thought to be the height of recession in motorcycle sales. But the company could not afford the indefinite postponement of a five year project involving R&D on such a scale and, having realised that the troubles in the motorcycle market lay, largely, with the bikes on offer, it saw no need. BMW was forthright in its condemnation of the Japanese, attributing the slack demand to public loss of confidence in the large motorcycle manufacturers "who have robbed many riders of the 'pleasure in riding' by irresponsible product and price policy." At the time of writing, sales of complex and impractical machinery, some of it suffering from inherent and incurable mechanical disorders and consuming tyres and chains and fuel at an excessive rate, continue to decline whilst sales of BMWs are on the increase. This would suggest that an accurate assessment of the market's needs rather than blind courage was behind the management decision to press ahead with the new models.

Interestingly, BMW's own sales figures had been suffering in 1983 and production was cut back by 10% but, with the benefit of hindsight, this was more than likely due to the failure of the ageing 'Boxer' models to attract new customers, a view borne out by the statistic that in the first six months of 1984 the K100RS and RT models were the best-selling motorcycles on the German market. 3878 were registered and sales were artificially depressed by the low secondhand value of Japanese machines and subsequent problems

Members of the factory's development team together with their handiwork in September 1983, just prior to the public launch of the K100.

K100 in action.

with part-exchanges. By the end of 1985 BMW had built 46,568 of the K-Series bikes and achieved their best sales figures ever.

As much of BMW's success depends upon its reputation for sound design and engineering a great deal of credit must be given to its advertising men. Not only have they created an 'up-market image' for the product and attracted into motorcycling the sort of status-conscious people you would normally expect to see peering through the tinted windows of expensive motorcars, but the orchestration of the introduction of the new machines was a nice example of their art, extracting as it did the very maximum amount of advertising 'mileage' from a series of well-staged events. First came the launch of the sleek but naked K100, very moderately priced in Britain to everyone's surprise at £3290. And this was followed by a round of dealer's 'viewing' parties and open-to-the-public test days. These, in turn, were followed at the end of 1983 by the announcement of the K100RS at the 'up-market' price of £4290 – the extra £1000 being asked, almost entirely, for the fairing – more showroom hype and more test days; the motorcycle press were invited to the South of France. Finally, in the Spring of '84, the K100RT with its sit-up-and-beg handlebars, touring fairing and a further modest increase on the price tag of £200, was dropped into our midst.

If the introduction of that stately lump, the Hesketh, caused quite a stir for rather different reasons, the reaction of motorcycle journalists to the K100 was unprecedented, especially as they were overwhelmingly in favour and, although the basic K100 did suffer somewhat in comparison with the elegantly faired K100RS, at £3290 it was pronounced to be a 'steal'.

We will look at press reaction in the form of road tests in another chapter, but one or two comments on the origins of the design are interesting. In a press release BMW had stated, categorically, that "No motorcycle in the world has ever had a longitudinally and horizontally mounted in-line engine" which, working on the premise that 'there is nothing new', may not seem very likely. A quick glance through the comprehensive tables at the back of *The Illustrated Encyclopedia of Motorcycles,* Irwin Tragatsch's monumental work that lists 2500 marques from 1894 up to the present day, would apparently bear out the truth of this surprising claim but 'Titch' Allen, writing in *Motorcycle Sport* in December 1983, came up with the information that, in 1959, Val Page had designed something very similar indeed for Ariel. The management of BSA, the parent company, had the prototype 'put down', which should come as no surprise to students of the death of Britain's motorcycle industry, but it still exists and can be seen in the National Motorcycle Museum – well worth a visit – situated close to Britain's National Exhibition Centre on the outskirts of Birmingham. Page had spent a lifetime in the motorcycle industry with J A Prestwich, Ariel, Triumph, BSA and back again to Ariel and his designs included the first vertical twin Triumph, the pre-war BSA Gold Star and the enclosed and innovative Ariel Leader. He loathed his greatest rival Edward Turner and Turner had no time for him – whenever Turner joined a company where Page was working Page immediately 'upped' and left – and

his experiences with Turner's Ariel Square Four had convinced him that any motorcycle that was intended to have several cylinders had best have them in line. Page's engine is a fan-cooled, push-rod, in-line four with a capacity of roughly 700 cubic centimetres. It has a single carburettor, a self starter – which at that time was most unusual – and the block is canted to one side providing a straight drive-line for a shaft to the rear wheel. In short, it bears a very close resemblance to BMW's own 'unique' design, but there is no reason to believe that anyone at BMW knew anything about it as, until quite recently, it was far from common knowledge even in Britain.

Crankshaft with toothed web for primary drive.

Above middle: **Transmission shaft of four-cylinder power unit.**

Above right: **Secondary shaft and clutch.**

Secondary shaft with disassembled damper.

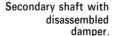

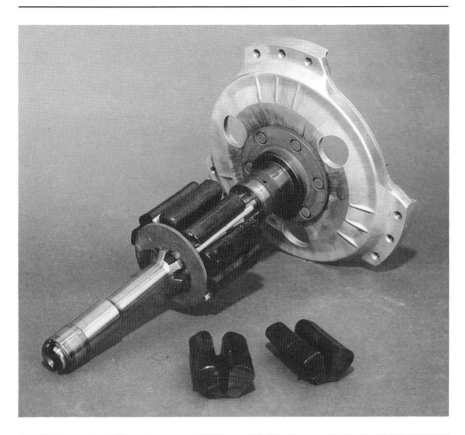

Secondary shaft with light alloy clutch carrier and damper.

Double function: Water pump (impeller) and oil pump (gearwheels) share the same housing.

BMW

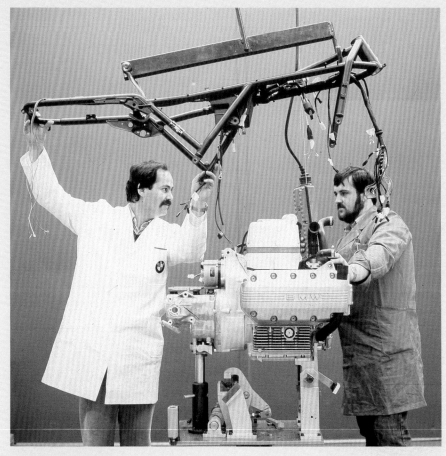

Engine and frame can be separated by loosening only five bolts and some electrical connections.

The Compact Drive System from both sides – illustrating the layout to perfection.

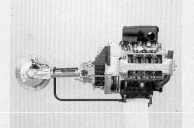

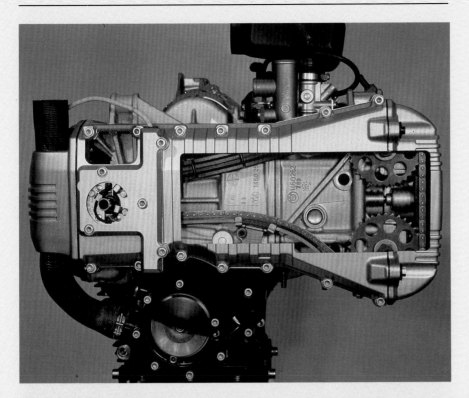

Front view of engine cut away to show timing chain, sprockets and tensioner.

Piston and crankshaft details exposed.

Fuel injection, ignition and valve gear details.

Not quite so tangible, but just as interesting, is journalist L J K Setright's inference, not claim, that the idea of laying the K100's engine on its side was his and not Herr Fritzenwenger's. Setright's theory of plagiarism was propounded in *Classic Mechanics* in a scholarly, if waspish article, highly critical of BMW, the K100 and Germany's 'Green-streaked and hypocritical society'. We shall return to his criticisms of the K100, but the bones of his complaint, put very briefly, are that in *Bahnstormer*, a history of BMW motorcycles which he wrote in 1976, he suggested that the 198cc R2 model of 1931, which had its single cylinder engine offset to the right in order to align the crankshaft to the drive shaft – 'the view from the left was very strange' – should have had its engine laid over on its side. 'The centre of gravity would be lower, the lateral balance better and access to the overhead valve gear and carburettor would be easier.

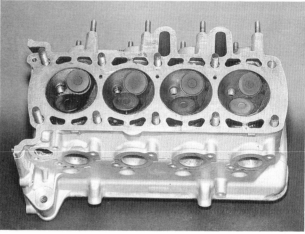

Light alloy engine block with four cylinders of 67mm bore.

Above right: Cylinder head, semi-spherical combustion chamber, squish area and valves lying in slightly different planes.

Really, it was only a matter of seeing what was obvious and I was amazed that BMW themselves had not seen it.' The book was published in 1977 and, according to the author, BMW took several copies so Fritzenwenger may have read it. The idea 'came to' Fritzenwenger, as Setright puts it, some time in 1978 – although BMW have stated that he thought of it the year before – and in 1979 he nipped down to the Munich Patents Office and registered the system. One must admit that it is possible that Setright gave him the idea. But then it is also possible that Setright, who has many contacts, knew of Page's in-line, laid-down four and the idea innocently surfaced as his very own when he was writing *Bahnstormer*, as indeed it may have bubbled up from Fritzenwenger's id when he was pondering the Peugeot engine. We shall never know unless Fritzenwenger, racked with guilt, confesses on his death bed.

The advantages of laying an engine on its side to drive a shaft are obvious enough. In fact, they are so obvious that it is surprising that this type of engine was not in common use some years ago, although the notorious conservatism of the motorcycling public may have had a lot to do with it. Whether the engine/gearbox/shaft drive

987cc four-cylinder, watercooled, fuel injected, 90bhp power unit with four stainless steel exhaust pipes.

unit patented as the BMW Compact Drive System was the brainchild of Val Page, L J K Setright, Josef Fritzenwenger, or the spontaneous result of a logical approach by three great minds, it is certainly a most effective package. BMW refer to it as a 'propelling backbone', which makes it sound a bit reptilian, but it is an accurate description as the CDS is central to the K100, both physically and intellectually, as Stefan Pachernegg's design team decided on the engine layout and arranged the rolling chassis round it.

BMW claim three particular advantages for its chosen layout, the first of which is that 'The low centre of gravity of the engine permits optimum handling and easy control of the machine'. Actually, the K100's C of G is not all that low, but that is not crucial

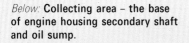

Below: **Collecting area** – the base of engine housing secondary shaft and oil sump.

Below right: **CDS** system – clearly showing engine assembly performing the vital task of stress member in the K-series frame design.

A K100 from the first production batch.

The five main bearings in the engine block.

to good handling at speed, although it helps at low speed and is a great help when one is manhandling a heavy bike.

The recumbent engine really scores on ease of maintenance and BMW is not slow to make the point that the twin overhead camshafts, the sparking plugs and the injection nozzles are easily accessible without having to take off the tank and, more importantly, that the crankshaft bearings, conrods and pistons can all be changed without having to remove the engine from the frame and laboriously taking it apart.

That 'The crankshaft installed longitudinally to the direction of travel permits direct drive to the drive shaft thus avoiding power losses as a result of deviations', which is the third advantage claimed for the CDS by BMW, is less convincing as the 5-speed box does not provide direct drive in any gear. This is one of the criticisms made by Setright in his analysis of the K100, although it is the claim of which he disapproves and not the deviations of the drive line, for the crankshaft drives a secondary engine shaft that takes power to the generator and the clutch and from the starter motor. And it is this secondary shaft with its contra-rotating clutch and generator that balances the torque reaction of the crankshaft. Torque reaction is the bugbear of BMW's flat twins and the contribution that this secondary shaft makes to the stability of the K-Series machines far outweighs the indirectness of the drive. Before we leave the subject, the forged steel crankshaft has five main bearings and balance weights on seven crank webs to ensure quiet running. The eighth crank web was designed as a spur gear and it is this that drives the secondary shaft that drives the single plate dry clutch, housed in an aluminium cage 7 inches in diameter which, in spite of its low weight, is effectively a flywheel.

The unfaired K100 weighs no more than 474lbs, only 4lbs more than a 1949 Series C Touring Vincent of much the same capacity.

This is as it should be, but it is very moderate by modern standards and from this it follows that, despite its bulk and liquid cooling, the Compact Drive System is extremely light. Chill cast – a sophisticated form of die casting – in an aluminium alloy containing magnesium and silicon, there are no cast-iron liners in the cylinders – a feature which it shares with the later air-cooled twins – and this keeps the dry weight down to 168lbs. Instead, the bearing surfaces of the alloy cylinders are treated with a nickel-silicon carbide abrasion-proof coating, called Scanimet, which reduces friction, improves heat transfer and allows smaller piston clearances for quieter running and better lubrication. These blocks cannot be rebored but should easily outlast the rest of the machine and sources independent of BMW confirm this with reports of no apparent wear at 130,000 miles.

Four valves per cylinder were considered at one stage of the design, but cost, weight saving and ease of maintenance were thought more important than excessive power. Two valves per cylinder, set at the relatively small angle of 19°, allow compact combustion chambers and the reasonably straight alignment of inlet and exhaust ports. A single roller chain drives the two camshafts, each supported on five bearings and this chain, which is situated at the front end of the engine, is easily accessible as a cam chain should be. Owners of CBX 550 Hondas will agree with that.

Something which surprised a lot of journalists, including Setright, is the omission from the engine of a balancing shaft to combat secondary vibration. All in-line fours vibrate to some extent but, because the K100's engine is mounted horizontally, the vibration is transmitted to the rider instead of being absorbed by the suspension as most of it would be with an upright in-line four. A balancer shaft with bobweights, located in the same plane as the cylinders and beside the crankshaft, would have damped out this vibration which, anyway, is not severe but this would have meant an even wider engine which at 504mm (19.8in) is already wide enough. However, the crankshaft is precisely counterweighted and two large dampers in the drive train – in front of the clutch and on the mainshaft of the gearbox – make a further contribution to suppressing the vibration.

The 987 cubic centimetres of the patented CDS are not extraordinarily potent when compared to those propelling all sorts of Oriental fours, but BMW had no intention of joining in a pointless power race. A nice balance between comfort, speed and handling is what they set out to achieve and 90bhp at 8000rpm is enough to push the unfaired K100 along at 133mph, more than adequate for the majority of riders, especially as it is almost twice the legal limit in most European countries. And the K100 will reach 60mph in 4.3 seconds, which is hardly sluggardly by any standards.

It may not be fashionable to say so, but there is nothing to be gained from high-revving engines other than the generation of enormous power, however nice they sound as they are wound up through the gears. What really matters in a road bike is not brutal power at fantastic revs per minute, but flexibility and power within the normal range of riding speeds, say 20 – 100mph. The K100 will trickle along at 20mph in top and pull away without transmission snatch. Impressive acceleration is available at quite low revs due to the engine's low speed torque – 57lbs/ft at 3500rpm – and at 100mph it is spinning over at 6000 revs. That means it is geared to roughly 20mph at 1230rpm and feels a little undergeared. It would be a nicer motorcycle at 20mph per 1000 revs but, in order to retain its flexibility and acceleration, that would require a bigger engine or a long-stroke engine with enormous torque, the outmoded route to high performance in a motorcycle engine. BMW has gone some way down that road, inasmuch as the K100 engine has a stroke of 70mm against a bore of 67. The contention is that the unusually long stroke is necessary in order to reduce the engine's length and keep the wheelbase within a reasonable 1516mm (59.7in) but a few millimetres either way would hardly make much difference and the long stroke may have been adopted to assist low speed torque.

The cooling and the lubrication systems are straightforwardly elaborate. The crossflow radiator is made of aluminium and there was a fair amount of heart searching, by computer, as to its ideal shape until somebody came up with the idea of using the traditional configuration of the BMW car grille. The coolant pump is housed in the same casing as the oil pump and, gear-driven by the front end of the output shaft, it circulates 2.8 litres of a 60/40 water/glycol mixture round the system. The alloy engine dissipates heat evenly and quickly, but an electric fan situated behind the radiator is switched on automatically when the coolant reaches 103°.

Lubrication is basically 'wet-sump', although the crankshaft is not allowed to splash about in oil as that would create unwanted heat and use up energy. Instead, the oil is contained in a compartment underneath the engine and a powerful pump, also driven by the output shaft, circulates it round the engine at 72 – 86psi, at a rate of 3500 litres every hour. The big ends and main bearings are all pressure fed; the hollow camshafts carry oil to their plain bearings; the cams and tappets are lubricated by oil pockets while the cylinders are lubricated by oil mist.

If all that sounds reassuringly 'low-tech' – on the grounds of the 'high-tech'/high cost equation that the customer must pay for – the fuel feed and ignition systems are controlled by an on-board digital computer. A manifestation of the supernatural to most motorcyclists but necessary for the efficient use of fuel, and to comply with emission control legislation. One cannot quarrel with the need for that, even if the thing 'malfunctions', which could mean a long walk home.

The four plugs, centrally placed in the combustion chambers, get their sparks from the control unit situated underneath the aluminium petrol tank. It not only keeps the ignition timing as a function of vacuum and engine speed, on a graph pre-programmed by exhaustive tests, but it also triggers the pulse for the solenoid valves of the fuel injection system, reduces the ignition advance to limit engine revs to approximately 8600rpm and switches off the injection process at 8750rpm, thus avoiding engine damage caused by over revving. Connected to the ignition system, the Bosch LE-Jetronic, used in hundreds of thousands of fuel injected BMW car engines, provides optimum fuel mixture. Installed in a safe place

K100 on test with *Motorcycle Enthusiast* magazine in late 1983.

beneath the seat, the LE 2 computer controls the quantity and duration of the injection, the quantity of air sucked in and the engine speed as a function of the temperature of the air intake and coolant. The exact quantity of fuel for all conditions not only leads to reduced fuel consumption, but to less air pollution from the exhaust. A fuel cutoff on the overrun provides additional fuel saving. Routine maintenance of the injection system is limited to a check-up of the idling synchronisation at 950rpm, but this can only be corrected using a workshop synchronizer across all four butterfly throttle valve adjusting screws. The fuel pump that feeds the fuel injection system lives in the 22 litre petrol tank.

Power for the lights and direction indicators is provided by an enormous alternator adapted from a BMW car generator, running at one and a half times engine speed, which has a 460 watt output – the later versions of the Ariel Square Four had a dynamo producing 70. This extraordinary power is more than sufficient for police use when radios, auxiliary lights, sirens and loudspeakers are required, often operating with the machine stationary and the engine at tickover.

The silencer is better than it looks. This is good news because it really is extremely ugly, but at least it is made of stainless steel and should not need to be replaced for years, which could be irritating if BMW come up with something better looking. There is an exhaust pipe in each corner, which explains the shape, all four being of equal length; the differences in their starting points are compensated for inside the 'box'. The design will not win prizes for artistic merit, but it should satisfy EEC noise abatement levels for some time to come.

The clutch is cable operated, but indistinguishable in 'feel' from a hydraulically operated clutch. Power is taken from it to the crown wheel and pinion at the rear stub-axle via the gearbox input shaft which drives the layshaft, which in its turn drives the mainshaft through a train of gears. The gearbox is separately lubricated and the gear selector mechanism is largely made of toughened alloy, the low inertia of the selector fork and the selector drum helping to improve the gearchange, hitherto not one of BMW's best features no matter what enthusiasts for the marque may say about it. Internal gear ratios are: 4.49, 2.95, 2.30, 1.87 and 1.66 to 1, the latter being top gear.

The gearbox mainshaft and final drive shaft are aligned and connected by a spline immediately ahead of the universal joint that compensates for the constant changes in drive shaft length caused by suspension travel. The drive shaft is in three sections: the first carrying the universal joint, the second section running 'dry' through a rubber shock absorber and the third section a splined stub shaft which connects directly with the pinion gear. The final drive ratio is 2.91 to 1 and the hub casing contains a sensor which transmits information to the electronic speedometer head.

The drive shaft runs from the gearbox to the crown wheel and pinion housing through the massive, L-shaped alloy 'Monolever', a one sided suspension system developed for the off-road BMW R80G/S flat twins which saves a lot of weight and makes for very easy wheel removal. The adjustable taper roller bearings carrying the 'foot' of the Monolever are attached not to the frame, but to the rear

Unpopular and ugly four-sided, stainless steel silencer was standardized for all the four cylinder models.

of the gearbox housing; a testimony to the faith of the design team in the rigidity of the aluminium structure.

At a fraction under 25lbs (11.3kg), the K100's frame is very light and simple as there really is not very much left for it to do, as it had shed most of the traditional responsibilities of a motorcycle frame to the 'propelling backbone' of the CDS which supports the rear suspension and provides the necessary rigidity to keep the wheels in line. The frame is little more than a convenient location for the top half of the single rear suspension unit and the bodywork, the radiator and the forks – which can easily be separated from the CDS by the removal of five bolts – and the severing of electrical connections by unplugging several plugs. Pachernegg has been quoted as observing that "Where high speed stability is involved, frame design is easy" and while the writers are not qualified to question such a statement, if this should be the case it does seem odd that very, very, few fast racing motorcycles handle really well. In the Agostini/Hailwood era the MV's handling was suspect and Hailwood's Honda 500 was appalling. Immense rigidity alone cannot guarantee complete stability and, while the K100 steers and handles very well in normal road use, aerodynamic factors will eventually upset its equilibrium.

There are a number of good reasons for the decision to continue using teledraulic forks on the K100, although in the 1950s BMWs made extensive use of very handsome Earles type items. They virtually eliminate fork 'dive' under heavy braking and fork trail is easily adjustable for sidecar use, but a K100 with a 'chair' would hardly be in keeping with the image that BMW have created for the bike. There are better front suspension systems – hub centre steering for example – but that would cost a fortune to develop properly and would be unaesthetic unless concealed inside a fairing which, on a bike of this height, would be difficult to do. 'Teles' work well and are quite attractive, their main drawback being a disconcerting walking movement of the legs when under stress. Experiments conducted by Fritz Egli, the Swiss frame builder, have proved conclusively that the only cure for this condition is a wheel spindle 65mm (2.5in) in diameter and that stout bracing by a bridge piece across the fork legs does no good at all. There are no fork braces on a K100, but the wheel spindle is only 25mm (1in) in diameter, although very strongly clamped to the bottom of each fork leg. Internally, the forks are very similar to those fitted to the 'Boxer' twins, with a travel of 185mm (7.3in) controlled by constant rate springs 395mm (15.5in) in length and double acting dampers with Teflon coated aluminium pistons. There are no arrangements for the adjustment of either springs or dampers, as BMW are quite convinced that they have arrived at the ideal compromise between ride quality and roadholding.

Apart from being 'one-sided', the rear suspension is conventional with one gas damped strut or 'monoshock' on the offside of the machine. This has a travel of 110mm (4.3in) and, while there are no provisions for the rider to control the degree of damping, spring tensions can be easily adjusted to one of three positions to compensate for variations in the load.

Neither is there anything unusual about the Brembo-manufactured braking system, except perhaps the quaint phrasing of a BMW press 'handout' referring to a 'brake dosage device' on the rear wheel. The twin stainless steel discs on the front and the single rear are all 285mm (11.2in) diameter. All three have semi-metallic pads and are hydraulically operated.

The cast light alloy wheels, with Y-shaped spokes of H-cross section, are unfashionably large and all the better for it visually.

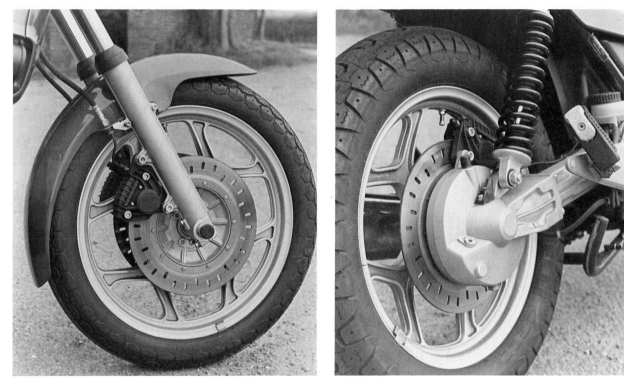

BMW experimented with smaller wheels, but came to the conclusion that an 18in front wheel gives a better 'contact patch' which enabled them to use a 63° steering head angle with a 105mm (84.1in) trail; a geometry that, for the K100, gives the best possible compromise between comfort and steering and handling at all speeds. The 17in rear wheel was chosen partly because it offered a more reasonable seat height of 810mm (31.9in) and ground clearance of 175mm (6.9in) and was yet another compromise, this time between wear and comfort. The transmission of a comparatively modest 60bhp to the road surface allied with sustained high speed can cause unacceptable wear problems, although 10,000 miles from the rear tyre of a briskly ridden K100 is not impossible.

The wheel rims are 2.50 – 18 MT H2 at the front and 2.75 – 17 MT H2 on the rear and they are designed for tubeless tyres; something new for BMW who in the past have never used them due to the difficulties of emergency repairs. They have now relented on the grounds that the slow deflation rate of a punctured tubeless tyre

Above left: **18-inch eight spoke cast alloy wheels, twin 285mm stainless steel discs and dual Brembo calipers.**

Above: **Single rear shock, rear drive casting and sturdy Monolever rear end.**

Instrumentation and switchgear. Rocker switches are for additional accessories.

Slogan in background reads; 'Fun for Everyone'. Unfortunately for BMW and its customers, the standard K100 did not fulfil all its expectations.

is a useful safety factor at the speeds for which the K100 was intended and Pirelli Phantoms, Michelins or Metzelers are recommended. The Pirellis are possibly the best for grip and the Metzelers the best for wear.

Footrests and handlebars are rubber mounted and, to a great extent, they insulate the rider from the vibration of the engine which, in any case, is never serious. Perhaps one should say pilot and not rider for the brochure lists 'cockpit' equipment. This includes an electronic speedometer and revolution counter, rear light indicator, a digital clock, a trip distance recorder with 100 metre graduations, fuel indicator light, coolant temperature warning indicator, digital gear indicator, direction indicator light and indicating lights for oil

British road racing champion Roger Burnett performing a K100 size wheelie. Proud owner is Grimsby BMW dealer, Harvey's.

pressure, alternator, headlamp full beam and choke, in addition to the usual, conventional, controls.

For what it is worth, if the digital gear indicator fails, blanking out the tiny screen, the bike can still be started by pulling in the clutch lever while pressing on the starter button. And the choke is rarely needed, except for starting on the very coldest winter morning.

All in all the K100 is a comprehensive and attractive package, even at the current price, but in 1983 some writers were suggesting that the Kawasaki GT750 was much better value and they had a point. For reasons of its own BMW had deliberately left undone things which it should have done and the basic version of the long awaited in-line four was not quite as good as a motorcycle as it might have been, as we shall see when we come to analyse the K100RS.

4

K 100RS

BMW has made a special point of stressing the uniqueness of its Compact Drive System, which is not quite as novel as it likes to think and, in the process, has rather under-played a more important claim to singularity. Since the motorcycle industry 'took off' at the turn of the century manufacturers have always gone to considerable trouble and expense to advertise the fundamental differences between their sports and touring models. The comfort, docility, economy and gentility of the latter contrasting sharply with the former's high lift cams, high compression heads and pistons, rock hard suspension, 'tuned' exhausts and all the other anti-social attributes intended to summon up the corpuscles – and money – of right-minded youths. This tradition has been largely followed by the Japanese who, having rubbed the Europeans' noses on the racing line of all the major circuits, have taken things a bit too far in the performance stakes for Governments to tolerate for long. Their Grand Prix look-a-likes are ideal scapegoats for the politicians in their public posturings about road safety. BMW has been highly critical of the escalating power race, but all the Japanese have done is to beat the European manufacturers at the game that they invented, although 160mph could be considered a bit 'quick' on the public highway. The 137mph of the K100RS model could equally be frowned on by the anti-motorcycle lobby, but it does not attract attention by looking like, or sounding like, a Grand Prix racer. All the K-Series bikes are extremely civilised machines, in a mildish state of tune and the point that BMW should make more strongly is that the 'cooking' K100, the sporting RS version and the luxuriously appointed touring models are mechanically identical. That really is unique.

Leaving aside the latest addition to the K-Series, the K100LT tourer, which has a radio, loudspeakers, aerials and other non-essentials that do nothing to improve its function as a motorcycle, the *only* major differences between the other three K100 models are the levels of protection, or the total lack of it. And the other differences are very minor, amounting to no more than a slightly higher axle ratio of 2.81 to 1, narrower handlebars, a digital quartz clock on the RS and a pair of high-rise handlebars on the RT.

The effect on the performance created by the different fairings, or even more marked by the lack of a fairing, is so extraordinary as to give the impression that one is riding, or reading road tests, of three totally dissimilar machines and leaves one wondering why BMW should bother with the unfaired K100 as the K100RS is so much nicer.

The official reason that the K100 is for "those who want to feel the breeze in their nostrils" – a 133mph 'breeze' would probably inflate their heads – is not at all convincing and was obviously thought up by somebody who has never had a cyclone howling through his nasal passages. As enthusiasts we do tend to overlook the simple fact that motorcycle manufacturers build motorcycles in order to make money, at least in theory. The real reason for the existence of the K100 has to be commercial and we have this from the horse's mouth. In a conversation with Stefan Pachernegg, printed in the February 1984 edition of *Motorcycle Sport,* Dave Minton asked him why BMW had not incorporated spoilers into the radiator cowling of the K100 as at speed it lacked the 'glued-down feel' of the 'aerodynamically stabilized RS model.' Pachernegg's

Rider's-eye view.

reply is interesting: "We could have done; some of us wanted it but then we decided that BMW needed what we call a 'poor bike'. We had to have something people could progress *from* so we intentionally designed one model of much lower price than the others and without any high speed aids or weathershielding. Ownership of that model will create ambition for the improved model just ahead. You understand?''

At the current price the K100 is hardly a 'loss leader' and BMW

Wind tunnel developed fairing permits not only riding at speed without wind pressure, but also increased stability.

can quickly quell any feelings of privation with the whacking £903 that it charges for the fairing of the K100RS – back in 1984 it was £1000 – less a few pounds for the digital quartz. While this fairing is not large and its effect in terms of speed is minimal, its effect on handling and comfort are profound and made a deep impression on the journalists who rode the early road test bikes. Almost everybody commented on the feeling of stability imparted by the K100RS, while they were critical of the high speed handling of its poor relation and the vibration that was transmitted to the rider through the nearside footrest.

Much of this vibration was caused by the mountings of the silencer, which have since been modified, but it was less noticeable on the RS model as the engine was, and still is, rubber-mounted on the two front engine bolts while the K100 engine was rigidly attached. BMW never mentioned this deliberate down-grading of the K100 and some journalists were so impressed with the RS fairing that they gave it credit for properties it never had and attributed the smoothness of the RS to it.

While BMW's R&D department has yet to make a fairing that will cure vibration, it is certainly responsible for the superb roadholding of the sports RS. And its top speed of 137mph, a very modest increase on the K100, would suggest that the primary

Some of the early design drafts for the K100RS fairing.

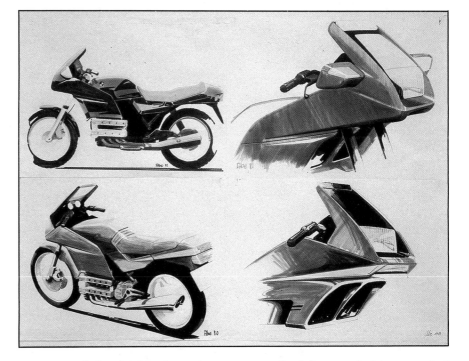

purpose of the fairing is to improve roadholding and rider comfort rather than top speed and this would be consistent with the policy of more than adequate performance allied to civilised road manners. After all, compared to other unfaired 'superbikes' there is very little wrong with the handling of the K100, which leads us to the thought that the suspect high speed handling of many Japanese machines of the 1970s might have been due more to poor aerodynamics than to design deficiencies in their chassis and suspension. And that it might not be possible to build an unfaired motorcycle that is stable at speeds much in excess of 130mph.

The elegant creation that clothes the K100RS is much smaller than the one designed for the twin cylinder R100RS twins some years ago, but it offers both improved performance and a good level of protection for the rider. And while the 1976 'full' fairing was developed in the draughty cavern of a wind tunnel hired from the Italian styling house of Pininfarina to help the engineers evolve the shape, the later fairing was perfected in BMW's own tunnel at the Spandau factory in Berlin. Unlike the 'wings' of racing cars which generate more grip by 'loading' of the tyres through downthrust, the 1980's RS fairing is designed to counter lift and does not exert a load, as BMW's experiments have proved the fairings shaped

Amazing what a fairing can achieve! Compare the rather conservative touring lines of the standard K100, to the aggressive sporting stance of the K100RS in the foreground.

specifically, or accidentally, to exert a load on the front tyre have unpleasant side effects when the vehicle is out of vertical. The down-thrust of the RS fairing that balances the front wheel's tendency to lift at speed – the factor which upsets the handling of the unclothed K100 – is provided by the windscreen area which is designed to be a spoiler. The lip beneath the radiator is another spoiler, calming an area of turbulence creating drag in the space between the front wheel and the engine.

Although designated as a sports machine, the RS is all things to all riders and such is the confidence conveyed by its near faultless handling that it makes an excellent long distance tourer, in the GT tradition, as quite daunting distances can be covered at high speed without undue fatigue. Protected from wind pressure and bad weather in the cockpit, the rider can adjust a spoiler at the top edge of the screen to divert the slipstream so that it does not batter at his helmet and the aerodynamically integrated mirrors, which also house the flashing indicators, protect the hands and keep them dry even in torrential rain. The holes through which the fork legs pass are sealed and insulated outlets carry away engine heat. The only drawback is the complete exposure of the rider's legs and feet which were well

Proving the RS can be a practical means of transport – even in adverse conditions.

protected by the cylinders and fairing of the R100RS, although in that design the face and helmet were more exposed.

At a dry weight of 225kg (496lbs) the K100RS is not significantly heavier than the K100 and while the fairing, which is made of plastic reinforced with fibre-glass, is responsible for the increase of 10kg, it more than pulls its weight, although it costs an awful lot of money and is responsible for almost one sixth of the current purchase price.

In 1986 BMW announced a limited edition, known as the K100RS Motorsport, in celebration of the fact that the K100RS had, for the third time running, been voted 'Motorcycle of the Year' by readers of *Motorrad*, the influential German motorcycle magazine. 120 machines were allocated to the UK market, all in Pearl metallic white with a purple, pink and turquoise stripe – which was nicer than it sounds – and windscreen, engine block and wheel rims all in black. They were mechanically identical to the standard model, but had the K75's fork bridge or 'stabilizer' and Pirelli radial tyres.

In 1987 the readers of *Motorrad* once again voted the K100RS as 'Motorcycle of the Year' – which made it four years running – and BMW marked the occasion by announcing a slightly over-done, all black, but with a grey seat covering, 'Special' version. With polished

Right: Testing the definitive design – a mini spoiler on the top of the windscreen can be swivelled to alter airflow angle.

Far right: K100RS fairing – the keynote of the model's sales success.

Technical 'exposure' illustration of K100RS.

B M W

1986 Limited-Edition K100RS
Motorsport. 120 were imported
into Britain selling
at £5078.

fins and 'pinstripe' edges this model has 'RS Style' in red and rather Japanese style lettering on each side of the fairing and the K75's 'Sporttuned' suspension, front and rear, with radial tyres at a surcharge of 12%.

While this is a surprisingly small increase on the price of the standard K100RS one might still be tempted to the view that BMW, like Porsche, have aimed their products at a sector of the market prepared to pay high prices for a fashionable image. To some extent that is true, although even at the 1988 price the K100RS has intrinsic value and makes good economic sense as a rapid transit system, for business or for pleasure, or as a 'macho' toy.

The Motorsport version was so
popular that 1987 saw BMW
produce another batch, this time
in black, with 'RS Style' in
contrasting red on each side of
the fairing.

5

K100RT and K100LT

Having looked, in some depth and detail, at the K100 and K100RS there is very little left to say about the K100RT, or its upwardly mobile stablemate the K100LT for, as we have already seen, the only major differences between the models are the fairings, or the lack of a fairing. However, there is a major difference between the fairings of the K100RS and the K100RT and the effect that these disparities exert upon the 'personalities' of otherwise all but identical machines is just as marked as the dissimilarities of the K100 and K100RS. Fit the sleek sports fairing to a K100 and it becomes the sleek and sporting RS model. Fit the wider, taller, touring fairing and it becomes the supremely comfortable and dignified RT/LT. You have the feeling that the fairings have been fitted to two entirely different motorcycles, although neither of them suffers from the tendency to front end aviation that mars the unfaired bike at high speed.

While the 'cockpit' of the K100RS protects the rider, or most of him or her from the slipstream and whatever is carried in it, the sports fairing could fairly be described as skimpy, but with the RT/LT fairing BMW have gone all-out for rider comfort and there are those who think they might have gone a bit too far. In doing so, they have divorced the rider from the road as well as from the elements and the impression is of riding on a two wheeled car.

There are also those, unlike us, who say that the RT's fairing is as aerodynamically effective as that of the RS, but that the fairing of the latter, the RS that is, offers better, safer protection than the touring fairing in really stormy weather. Road testing cannot be regarded as a branch of science – it may be less objective than we like to think – but I (Mick Walker) tested a K100RT during a severe October gale. While the K100RS retains its 'stuck down' feel in such conditions, the RT's response to strong sidewinds was worrying, but, in heavy rain the RT fairing kept the rider drier than the RS fairing, especially around the feet and legs. I would stress 'the rider', for on both the RS and RT/LT the rider has the lion's share of protection, while the pillion passenger is a great deal more exposed.

'Aerodynamically optimized' is the awful phrase the brochure uses to describe the RS fairing, but it makes no such claim for the fairing of the RT/LT which would suggest that it, or rather they, are less aerodynamically effective. Road test performance figures would seem to bear out this conclusion, giving a top speed for the K100RT between 1 and 9mph slower than the K100RS, depending on who did the testing. Interestingly, the latest BMW brochure does not claim any particular top speed for any of the K100-Series, merely stating 'Maximum speed over 200km/h (123mph)'. Fuel consumption figures also lead one to the same conclusion. BMW claim 45mpg for the K100; 49.7mpg for the K100RS, and 48.1mpg for the K100RT, all calculated at a steady 75mph. Most road test claims for motorway conditions are very similar indeed.

Factory styling draft.

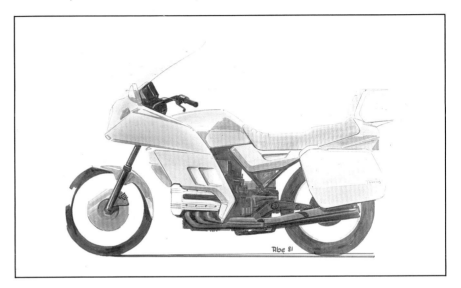

Unlike the K100RS fairing, the RT/LT version is wider than the engine and extends below it, giving full protection for the rider's legs and feet. But that also means it is a bit slab-sided and it might be this that causes sensitivity to sidewinds. Being that much bigger than the RS fairing – it is 116mm (4.5in) wider and 5kg (11lbs) heavier – it should not come as a surprise to learn that it is even more expensive. £110 in fact, or exactly £10 for every pound in fairing weight. In the 1950s it was possible to estimate, with a fair degree of accuracy, the price of almost any British bike from its given weight. There has to be a correlation between weight and price. For example, the dry weight of a K100RT was 230kg (506lbs) and the December 1987 price was £5629 which gives you £11.12 per pound. The K100RS works out at £10.95 and the hefty K100LT at £10.58 per pound in weight. The unfaired K100 price/weight ratio of £9.61 per pound confirms what everyone suspected; BMW fairings are exceedingly expensive. But BMW will justify its prices by saying, quite truthfully, that its fairings are scientifically designed, beautifully constructed in heavy gauge material and superbly finished.

Of the first three K100 models, the consensus of informed opinion is that the K100RS is the best in every way, with the exception of protection from really foul weather and, even on that aspect, the RT's advantages are marginal and are offset in other ways. The only thing about the RT that everyone preferred were the glove compartments in the fairing.

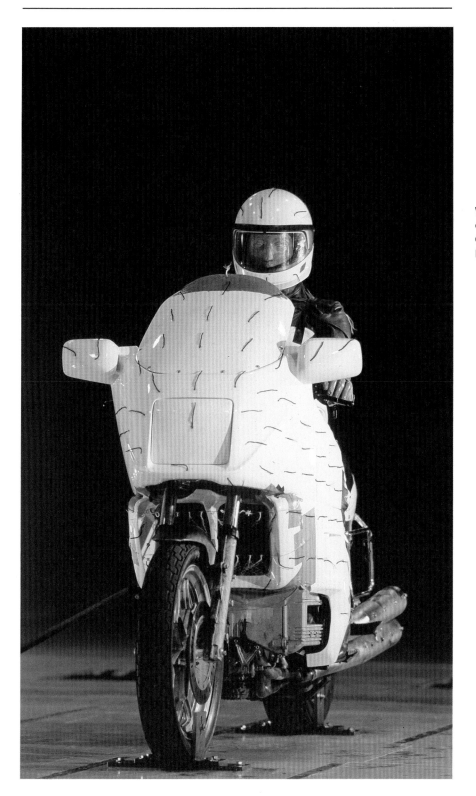

Wind tunnel testing to achieve optimum fairing shape – note double-barrel silencer of this early prototype.

B M W

K100RT. Launched in 1984, the third K-Series models followed the K100 and K100RS versions. Panniers were standard equipment.

Front and rear views of RT illustrate the comprehensive protection afforded to the rider.

The RT can take its rider almost anywhere in comfort – and with a high level of protection from the elements.

Fairing in more detail – it tends to
divorce the rider from the road.

Normally, one should take such opinions with a fair amount of
salt. Motorcycle journalists, however knowledgeable, are not to be
relied upon when it comes to the question of which bike *you* ought
to buy. They rarely take into account such things as running costs,
reliability and resale value and some of the bikes they have chosen to
be 'Bike of the Year' have been a joke, provided that you did not buy
one. And motoring journalists are just as bad in this respect.

However, in this case they have been proven to be right. The
K100RS will do anything that its broader showroom mate will do
and do it faster, with less effort, on a bit less fuel. That being the case
the K100LT, which is a luxurious version of the K100RT, might seem
a bit extraneous, but for the existence of the Honda Aspencade.

The late, great Dennis May once remarked that the post-war Harley Davidson V-twin was an amusement arcade and not a motorcycle. The Aspencade weighs a third of a ton and costs over £8000 – a price to weight ratio of £11.17 to 1 – and it is a pity that dear old Dennis did not live to see one. Nevertheless, there are a lot of them about, which proves there is a ready market for such things

and BMW have aimed the luxurious LT at the Aspencade's red neck in a bid to grasp a slice of it.

An RT rider stops to consult his map whilst touring in France.

One could describe the KL100LT as a civilised version of the Aspencade without the onboard fruit machines. At a dry weight of 259kg (569.8lbs) it is comparatively slim and at £6885 it is comparatively cheap; and the price includes the panniers, as it does for the RT.

The price also includes a special golden finish, which BMW describe as 'Bahama bronze metallic', a black engine block with polished ribs, 'high-comfort' seat in pearl-beige, integrated radio and speakers, additional power sockets, aerial, suppressors, emergency flasher unit and Nivomat self-levelling rear suspension.

The prop stand and the centre stand with its foldaway grab handle are all standard items and it says a lot for their designer that it is possible, without any undue strain, to pull any of the K-Series machines up on to the centre stand. However, caution is required, as a combination of a wet boot and a wet stand peg can prove very slippery and it is not difficult to drop the bike.

What owning an RT is all about –
sea, sun and scenery.

For serious long distance touring both the K100RT and LT are supremely practical mounts, offering a rare combination of comfort, performance, relatively low weight, rider protection and carrying capacity. But it takes some time to get accustomed to the seemingly huge fairing.

Luxury variant, the K100LT with its additional accessories and Bahama bronze metallic paintwork. In cost terms, the top of the K-Series range, the new K-1 Super Sportster excepted.

Cockpit of LT showing radio, twin speakers and additional instruments.

6

K75

The K75 was launched in Austria during September 1985 and this official introduction occasioned some surprise which was itself surprising, for a 3-cylinder BMW had been photographed on test in Germany as long ago as the summer of 1983, before the introduction of the K100. Reports and pictures of the new machine were featured in the press and Dr Eberhardt Sarfert, the Chairman of BMW, publicly 'came clean' and admitted its existence.

The introduction closely paralleled that of the K100, in so much as BMW was launching a new bike which, in the eyes of some hard-riding journalists, was far from perfect. Criticism largely centred on what was thought to be soft and under-damped suspension, but the K75C was designed to be a tourer with a comfort over handling priority and was not another illustration of the firm's 'poor man's motorcycle' policy. In spite of these shortcomings, which were supposed to cause the bike to gently weave if pressed very hard through bumpy bends, there were quite a few 'poor men' prepared to stump-up £3750 and, within a month, the new model had captured 7% of the British 750cc market. Many people who had just bought K100s wished they had had a chance to try a 'three'.

The second 750, the K75S, virtually a 3-cylinder version of the K100RS, made its debut in June 1986 and the range was further strengthened at the Cologne show of that year with the introduction of the unfaired K75 – up-market rather than down-market – and a 'limited edition' K75S Special or K75SS.

All four versions of the three are mechanically identical, but there are quite major variations in the fairings, suspension rates, rear brakes and rear wheel sizes. For the most part the engine is literally three quarters of the 987cc K100-Series engine with a capacity of 740cc, but using a modified R80 clutch and straight-cut gears to drive the secondary shaft which sound as though a family of owls has nested in the engine. The most significant dissimilarity is the addition of the contra-rotating balance shaft, which runs at engine speed beneath the crankshaft and virtually eliminates the vibration inherent in an in-line three.

In-line 'threes' promise perfect balance, but the pistons which are unavoidably out of phase set up a 'rocking couple' almost on the scale of a 180° twin of similar capacity and such twins are notoriously rough. These forces can be counteracted to a large extent in an in-line 'four' by arranging things so that the two end pistons are at top dead centre while the two middle pistons are at the bottom of the stroke. Nevertheless, the K75-Series 'threes' are considerably smoother than the K100-Series in-line 'fours'.

Apart from the K75's lower axle ratio of 3.2 to 1, the only major differences are the shorter inlet manifolds, the new shapes for the piston crowns and the combustion chambers, raising the compression ratio from 10.2 to 1 to 11 to 1, and a modified and better looking silencer – still in stainless steel – with three sides instead of four. These departures from the design of the 4 cylinder engine lead to a proportional power increase of 7.5bhp, the total output being 75bhp at 8500rpm against the 90bhp of the in-line four. Bore and stroke remain the same and torque is excellent with 50.37lb/ft available at 6750rpm – in fact, 83% of torque 'on tap' at 2500rpm – and the threes will pull away quite happily from 30mph in top.

In spite of the proportional power increase and smoother power delivery, the rider who wants power at the top end of the performance range will prefer one of the K100-Series. And he will not suffer much financially from such a choice as the differences in the prices of the threes and fours are not all that significant. In late 1987, the K75C at £4238 was only £318 cheaper than a basic K100 and the K100RS costs only £840 more than the £4689 asked for its three quarter engine size equivalent, the K75S. The cost of fuel is not a serious consideration, for BMW itself claims no more than a 4% reduction in consumption for the smaller bikes which, broadly speaking, means 49-53mpg, ridden hard.

Top speeds are not earth-shaking in current terms, but 124mph for the K75C and 130mph for the sportier K75S and variants will be more than fast enough for some owners, if they are honest. Speeds in the first four gears are 45, 68, 88, 107 respectively and independent road tests give acceleration figures for the K75S that vary between 13.1 and 13.77 seconds for the standing quarter mile. 0-60mph is possible in 4.3 seconds, exactly the same time claimed for the K100RS, but for most owners the results of such brutalities are neither here nor there.

The K100-Series frame, suitably modified to take the shorter engine, is employed on all four versions of the three cylinder machines which share the 1516mm (59.7in) wheelbase of the K100s. The forks fitted to the K75C and the later K75 are the standard item, but those of the K75S and K75SS differ radically, internally, with two springs in each fork leg, but with a double-acting hydraulic damper in the left leg only. They have also had their fork travel considerably reduced from 185mm (7.3in) to 135mm (5.3in) in keeping with their sporting image. This notable departure from the suspension norm of the K-Series is called 'Sporttuning' and it is now available for the K100RS, at £84 extra, while the standard long travel 'comfort' suspension, front and rear, is optional for the K75S and K75SS.

Interestingly, the fork legs of all four 'triples' have bracing pieces bridging the front mudguard. These are catalogued as 'external fork stabilizers' and would suggest that the large fork spindle is not large enough to stop the legs from 'walking', but whether or not they do

The frame of the K models had to be modified around the front supports for the smaller power plant.

have much effect is open to discussion. As already mentioned, Fritz Egli's teachings plainly state that fork braces contribute nothing whatsoever to stability and it is possible that they have been re-introduced at popular request.

The 'Monolever' rear suspension system with its single gas damped strut, adjustable to three positions of pre-load, is identical to that of the K100-Series, excepting that the 'Sporttuned' units fitted to the K75S and SS models are more heavily damped and have a slightly shorter travel than the 110mm (4.3in) of the standard strut.

The plastic cover that conceals the rear wheel nuts of the K100s is not fitted to the triples. This makes it very difficult to clean this area and, as the cover costs no more than £4 including VAT, it seems a strange economy. Another minor criticism is the single horn which is a pathetic thing compared to the twin horns of the K100s.

At 810mm (31.9in), unladen seat height is also identical to the K100, which suits tall people very nicely but is the cause of some annoyance to shorter riders. K75s may be fairly light machines by modern standards with a dry weight of only 204kg (448.8lbs) – the K75S and SS versions weigh a little more, 11kg to be precise – but this is still a lot of weight to manoeuvre at low speeds if your feet do not touch the ground. The seats, like those fitted to the later K100s, are not so deep as the original design and slightly firmer, although in

View showing just how much shorter and compact the 3-cylinder engine is compared to its bigger brother.

our experience they are extremely comfortable, even on long journeys.

Rear wheels and rear wheel braking systems also vary between the four machines. The K75S and SS sport the standard 17in K100 wheel with its single stainless steel disc brake, while the K75 and 75C have a 2.75 – 18 rear wheel with a single 200mm (8in) drum brake, which is more than adequate for rear wheel braking, especially in wet conditions. The standard K-Series double-disc front brakes are fitted to all models.

Like the K100s, the four K75s vary in the degree of protection from the weather that they offer, the K75 having none at all. The

Equalizing shafts without a damper proved superior to the prototype method, particularly in the design shown here with two weights.

With the crankpins disposed at an angle of 120°, the crankshaft of the 3-cylinder had various counterweights to improve overall balance. A helical drive gear connected with the drive shaft in the oil sump was also tested in addition to the spur gear used on production engines.

The K75C got its slimmer looks from the narrower radiator and its slender cover, 4cm (1.6'') smaller than the K100's. Shown here is the definitive design for production models.

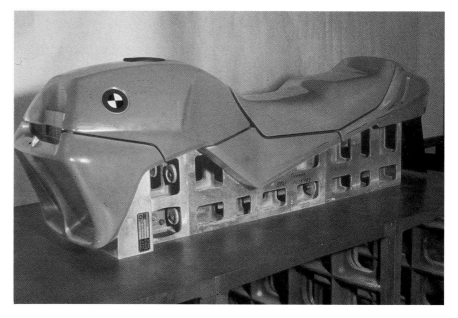

As a result, the supports of the smaller radiator had to be modified. For testing purposes, the radiator was provisionally welded to the frame.

The engine of a K75 being scanned by a 3D measuring machine. The dimensions thus determined were stored in a computer and could be used later.

Individual components of the K75 engine.

B M W

K75C, the first of the three-cylinder models to be offered, went on sale in September 1985.

K75C with a small windscreen perched upon a skimpy, rather Japanese, fairing that surrounds the headlamp does not offer very much, but a large handlebar-mounted windscreen can be ordered at no extra cost. The K75S has a much more effective fairing along the lines of the K100RS, but with no protection for the hands, while the K75S Special shares the upper half with the addition of a spoiler underneath the engine, giving the illusion of having a full fairing.

None of these creations is half as good as the fairing of the K100RS and its 'Motorsport' derivative and it is possible that the windscreen of the K75C may upset the steering. Certain roadtesters of the early versions of the bike complained of unpleasantly light steering but, as the front suspension set-up and geometry are exactly those of the extremely stable K100RS, one must look for other reasons not connected with these factors. It was originally intended that the K75C should not have a fairing but, remembering the comparative unpopularity of the unfaired K100, BMW's management relented and authorised a windscreen and it is this half-hearted effort that springs to mind as a possible cause of the complaints.

Left: Touring triple, the C provided an upright riding stance.

Computer-aided design was applied by BMW engineers in developing the streamlining for the sporting K75S.

Particularly as it is mounted on the handlebars and not the frame, although the screen is said to have been shaped in the Berlin wind tunnel and is apparently designed to exert some downward force to discourage lift and to counteract a 47/53% weight bias to the rear.

Whether or not the screen exerts sufficient downward force has not been documented, but BMW's solution to the problem was uncharacteristically crude, taking the somewhat make-shift form of a silicon-based damper block *inside* the steering head, bearing on the steering tube and inhibiting free movement. This strange device is called a 'Fluid block' and it is not inserted in the steering heads of any of the other K-Series machines. As with the K100RS, the fairings of the two 'quicker' versions of the K75 impart a sporting character but, while the fairing is entirely responsible for the K100's transformation, this is not quite the case with the two three cylinder machines as their 'Sporttuned' suspension makes its own substantial

Left: American film star Pierce Brosnan with the K75C which he rode in the film *The Fourth Protocol.*

contribution to stability at speed. Unfortunately, the fairings do not contribute quite as much to comfort, especially at speed and, above 70mph, taller riders are subjected to considerable buffeting around the head and shoulders. The engine spoiler of the K75S Special, which is available as an accessory, does nothing to protect the rider, although it may improve stability.

The riding position of all four 'threes' is basically the same, with footrests in the same, correct, relationship to the seat some little way behind its 'nose'. The handlebars do vary, with sit-up-and-suffer-at high-speed type touring bars on the K75 and K75C and elegant

Offside view of K75C, showing small handlebar-mounted fairing and radiator cover to advantage.

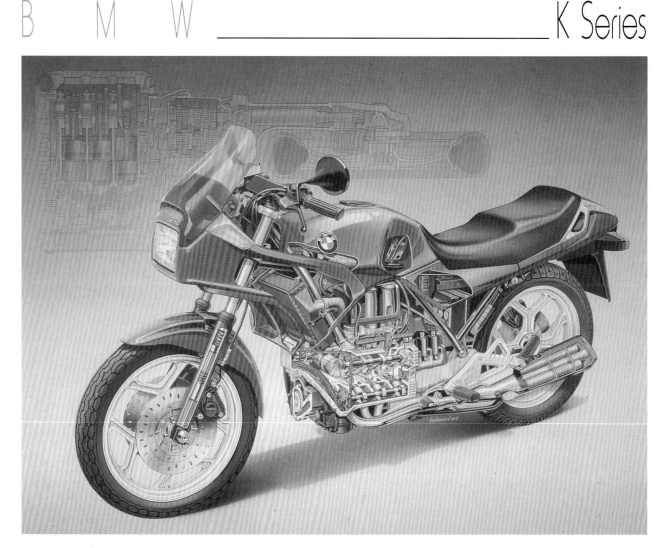

Design details of K75S exposed.

Right: With the road as its backdrop, this **K75S** looks the part. First available in June '86.

narrow bars that offer a more comfortable and ergonomically superior stance to riders of the sports machines. Instrumentation is identical on all K-Series bikes.

Bearing in mind the somewhat unenthusiastic welcome that was accorded to the unfaired K100, it does seem rather strange that BMW should choose to introduce a naked 'triple' to supplement the range. It was not significantly cheaper than the K75C; most of the difference accounted for by the unattractive little windscreen. Unlike the K100, there is nothing of the poor relation about the K75 which, according to the brochure, is aimed at 'motorcycle purists' who presumably enjoy being soaked or frozen or covered with squashed flies. But, to be fair, it also sensibly points out that the bike is ideal for those who wish to make their own arrangements with proprietary fairings. Although it is the least expensive model in the entire K-Series range, it is one of the most handsome with polished alloy fork legs and a chrome-plated headlamp and luggage rack. It has a bright red seat and the tank, tail section and the engine are in BMW's traditional glossy black, with red coach lining.

The K75S Specials also had a striking finish, at a fairly striking price of £4926 (late 1987), for which you got the engine 'spoiler', onyx black paintwork, with a black engine block and a pearl beige seat. Or a 'brilliant' silver finish, with black engine and monolever unit and a black dualseat.

The differences in character between the threes and fours are easily defined. Due to their lighter weight the threes are a much more

Left: **K75S** with engine spoiler, first offered as an optional extra in Autumn 1986.

Cockpit of **K75S**. Not only was the fairing a vast improvement over the K75C, but a digital clock was standard equipment.

Left: **K75S** made its debut at the Cologne Show in September 1986. Available in either black or silver, it sported the belly pan as standard equipment plus all-black engine, wheels – and monolever on silver version (illustrated).

sporting motorcycle, encouraging the rider to take a more spirited approach. And this feeling is accentuated by the engine. It feels more lively than the four which, because of its tremendous torque, is almost 'muscle-bound' and seems to need another, higher, gear between 50 and 60mph, while vibration levels are much higher up to 80mph. The three cylinder unit also revs more freely.

Also making its debut at Cologne in '86 was the base K75 model (left). Pictured here with a K75S Special.

Cheapest K – the K75. Even so, it is an attractive machine with black paintwork, red seat, polished fork legs and chromed headlight, seat carrier and complete silencer – including heat shield.

Like all the K-Series BMWs, the K75s are equipped with an emergency repair outfit for the tubeless tyres, a comprehensive and well written handbook and a generous tool kit of remarkably good quality. The tool kits that most manufacturers supply are tawdry nonsense, but such thoroughness is typical of BMW. Durability is the keystone of their manufacturing philosophy and to a great extent justifies the prices which have risen steadily since the launching of the K100 in October 1983.

The K75S now costs £5393 and out of all the K-Series BMWs it is probably the best; best being defined as most suited for its purpose, although the poor performance of the fairing in the comfort stakes, at least for taller riders, does let it down a bit. If only one could buy it with the K100RS fairing!

According to a press report, sources inside BMW have revealed that a turbo-charged K75 is being developed by the company, but BMW have denied that this is so. *Motor Cycle News* for 30 September, 1987 quotes Director Dietrich Maronde as saying: "There are definitely no plans for a turbo-charged K75 – it wouldn't fit into the model range". Nevertheless, Director Maronde went on to say that BMW "were working on all kinds of developments in all kinds of directions" and these developments could well include a turbo-charged machine.

The engine design and layout of the K75 unit lends itself to turbo-charging and such a development would put the company firmly in the forefront of the high performance stakes, although BMW have been highly critical of just that sort of thing. However, if experience with cars should count for anything in the context of a turbo-charged K-Series bike, then BMW can do it. The Japanese have flirted – and apparently failed – with turbos, leaving the way open for someone else to get it right. Which makes one wonder if the story could be more fact than fiction.

7

Latest Developments

BMW's new bikes for 1988 were announced in mid-September 1987, in a curiously worded press release from BMW AG which stated that the new versions of the K100 and K75 would 'presumably be available' respectively in January and February 1988. A display of indecision not usually associated with the company, but *presumably* brought on by the failure of the ABS to behave itself and meet the launch date.

The new models are mechanically identical to the existing range. The most noticeable development being the changes to the K100, which BMW describe as a down-to-earth, no-fairing, grassroots model. According to the press release: "Purchasers have shown a growing interest recently in 'basic' machines without a fairing. The genuine enthusiast riding a chopper, cruiser, or muscle bike wants to feel the wind racing past and see the technical features his motorcycle has to offer." Whether he would want to do both things at once is not made clear, but it seems more likely that the upsurge of interest in 'basic bikes without a fairing' could be attributed to the comparatively low cost of 'after-market' fairings compared to BMW's own product.

The facelift for the K100 comprises alterations to the radiator cover and the headlight cover, while the headlight, the exhaust shield and the front brake line sleeves are all chrome-plated. The engine cover, wheels and footrest plates are painted black and the edges of the fins are polished. Finished in Marrakech red, the K100 now has the 21 litre fuel tank of the K75, with integrated knee pads and side covers. The new high, wide and dreadful handlebars are by far the bike's worst feature, especially when allied to the new and markedly split-level seat. Alternative seat heights of 29.9 or 31.5 in (760 or 800mm) will be available; in itself, a good idea for shorter riders, but the bars and low seat height between them will dictate an ape-like and impractical position most uncharacteristic of a BMW.

The K100RS soldiers on unchanged, with the option of the sports-tuned suspension of the K75S, a solo seat in black or red and an engine spoiler. 1988 colours are brilliant-silver, red-metallic or Avus-black.

The K100RT is very little changed, except in price and range of colours which will be red-metallic, Bermuda-blue and stratos-grey. But the K100LT, the touring flagship, has a new, more upright

K100 was given its first real update since its 1983 launch for the 1988 season. Changes included bright silencer, lower seat height, black engine castings and wheels and higher handlebars.

1988 re-vamp endowed the base K100 with a totally fresh riding stance, far more laid-back than the original.

windscreen available in high or low versions. The former is 22 inches (560mm) in height and can be ordered with, or without, side flaps, while the low version is 16.9 inches (430mm) high. Only the low version without side flaps will be available in Germany as, under German law, a rider must be able to look over the windshield.

Other alterations will include an additional instrument panel behind the screen and above the standard set of instruments. This comprises gauges indicating the temperature of fuel and coolant, a map reading light, a socket and a cigar lighter. A larger topcase that will accommodate two helmets and double as a backrest will also be available. The Bahama-bronze metallic finish continues for another year.

In addition to the three 4-cylinder machines already mentioned, a new Special Edition of the K100RS has been introduced. The new model features mother-of-pearl white and Bermuda blue two-tone paintwork, white cast-alloy wheel with blue pinstriping and a blue engine spoiler and double seat. The windscreen is tinted black and the engine and the drive-train are finished in black with BMW picked out in white. The exhaust cover is chrome plated.

For 1988 the top-of-the-range LT was offered with an optional modified windshield, an additional instrument panel and a large top case with backrest.

B M W

Cockpit of 1988 LT, showing radio, twin speakers, switches and additional instruments.

Right: For 1988, the K75S Special was dropped from the BMW lineup. However, the K75S was uprated to SS specification and an additional colour, Marrakech red, was offered.

Other features include an automatic side stand, Pirelli radial tyres and sports-tuned suspension. Panniers with the lids finished in the mother-of-pearl paintwork are an option.

Like all the K100 series, the Special Editions are available with the newly-introduced ABS anti-lock braking system which is being marketed at cost for an extra £595. Only 60 of these machines have been imported into Britain, 30 of them with the ABS.

The K75-Series bikes will be offered in three versions instead of

Like the K100, the 1988 base K75 was made available with a lower seat measuring only 760mm (29.9 inches) in height. A particular advantage for the shorter rider.

four. The K75S Special has, apparently, been dropped but, in fact, it has assumed the less exciting title of K75S while retaining all the Special's extra features. So, in effect, it is the K75S as it used to be that has been dropped, except in designation. Colours are those that were offered for the Special, but with the addition of Marrakech-red, with a black seat and black drive train.

The K75C is unchanged for 1988 and will be on sale in Avus-black or henna-red. But some alterations have been wrought upon the K75 which, according to the advertising, is inexplicably intended as a status-symbol for 'achievers'. Although, *presumably*, under- or even non-achievers will be allowed to buy them, provided they can find the money. The distinctive black paintwork will be retained for 1988, but with bright blue plug leads and the rather unattractive dual level, clip-on, low seat is offered as an option for 'achievers' with short legs.

For 1989 model year the K75C and K100RT have been discontinued.

United Kingdom prices in December 1988 were . . .

K75	£4530
K75S	£5393
K100	£5272
K100RS	£6175
K100RS Special Edit.	£6450
K100LT	£6885

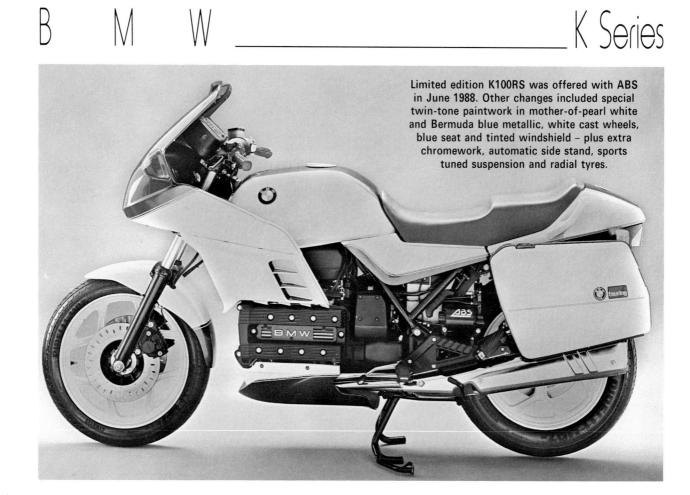

Limited edition K100RS was offered with ABS in June 1988. Other changes included special twin-tone paintwork in mother-of-pearl white and Bermuda blue metallic, white cast wheels, blue seat and tinted windshield – plus extra chromework, automatic side stand, sports tuned suspension and radial tyres.

Proof positive: BMW's ABS works . . .

8

K1–Super Sports

With the hi-tech K1, BMW have at last entered the super sports market. Launched at the Cologne Show in September 1988, the stunningly styled superbike – featuring four valves per cylinder – is the company's two wheel version of their exotic semi-experimental cars. The M1 was BMW's first coupe super car with the new Z1 launched in mid October 1988 the latest push at boundaries of car design.

As the old saying goes, standing still means stagnation. Even when introducing the K100 and K75 model series, therefore, BMW started to consider the future of the K-generation, the Company's engineers and stylists presenting the stage of model development on their drawing-boards. The task was clear. As in the first stage when developing the K-generation, the purpose of this second step was to move into another important segment of the market currently not occupied by BMW. Accordingly, BMW is now moving over from its classical touring machine segment to the super sports segment that has become increasingly significant in recent times.

This does not mean however that BMW is giving up old principles and participating in the "power race". So considerations other than simply power output were necessary.

To achieve this goal, one necessity was to make the running gear, brakes and fairing a perfect match for the increased power of the engine. And taking up BMW's heritage, it was indeed obvious that the fairing had to be further improved and streamlined to an even higher standard. After all, back in 1976 BMW introduced the R 100 RS, the world's first truly successful production motorcycle with full fairing that even today still reflects the state of the art in motorcycle engineering. The brief now given to BMW's designers, engineers and wind tunnel experts was to develop a new fairing further improving on the excellent streamlining of the K100RS, at the same time offering a new standard in the sports motorcycle market in terms of efficient protection in wind and weather and optimum riding stability at all speeds.

At the same time the new concept had to retain BMW's well-known virtues such as optimum ergonomics, superior riding comfort (including the passenger), ease of service, economy and a long running life.

Another task given to BMW stylists Klaus-Volker Gevert and

Launched at the Cologne Show in September 1988, the K1 is a four-valve high-performance model, with which BMW aim to grab a share of the 'ultimate in exclusivity' market – as they have done with cars such as the M3 illustrated.

K1 is a radical departure from BMW's usual conservative image.

Karl Heinz Abe and their team was to take up the unique, functional design of the K 100 Series, combining it with new features to give the new motorcycle new style and a unique appearance in line with its sporting image.

Development of an even more dynamic and sportier four-cylinder engine started back in 1983, the year the K100 was launched. BMW's strategy of progress was clear from the outset, since the four-valve principle had already been accepted worldwide as pacemaker of progress.

Martin Probst, the Head of Engine Development of BMW Motorrad GmbH, therefore set the Company's sights at further improving the K-concept. Coming from BMW's four-wheel Motorsport GmbH, he already had ample experience with four-valve engines considering that BMW's motorsport subsidiary had already converted a standard four-cylinder power unit into the World Champion Formula 1 engine.

While the ultimate objective in Formula 1 was obviously to achieve maximum engine output, the task of BMW's motorcycle engineers in developing their four-valve engine was also to observe BMW's heritage in achieving an even higher standard of riding culture, practical everyday value, economy and a long running life.

The engineers' task was to improve the engine above all in terms of torque and output throughout the entire speed range, thus making it superior to the two-valve unit in every respect. Obviously, therefore, the objective was to reach – but intentionally not exceed – the output limit of 100 bhp (74 kW) agreed voluntarily by all motorcycle manufacturers in the Federal Republic of Germany.

Following the presentation of the first road-going prototype, the Board of Management of BMW AG gave the project their go-ahead in September 1986. Now the development of the new machine was able to start full swing. Precisely two years later, the result of this efficient development process was presented to the public for the first time at the International Bicycle and Motorcycle Exhibition in Cologne in September 1988.

A comparison of the K100 and K1 output and torque curves shows that the new four-valve power unit has reached these objectives in every respect.

Engine output is up from 90 to 100 bhp (in both cases at 8000 rpm), torque has been increased from 86 Nm (63ft/lb) at 6000 rpm to 100 Nm (74ft/lb) at 6750 rpm.

With the K1 BMW have set out to refute the claim that four-valve power units are inflexible and unrefined by nature. They believe the more sophisticated design of the engine with twice the usual number of valves providing a faster, more efficient and dynamic cylinder charge also serves to improve the combustion process and increase the gas flow at low and medium engine speeds. The mean operating pressure of the K1 power unit, which is often regarded as a yardstick for determining the design quality of an engine, is a very healthy 12.7 bar.

This new design concept is claimed to greatly improve the running smoothness of the BMW four-cylinder, despite the increase in engine output. The rider can therefore achieve even better performance and higher road speeds without constantly needing to change gear as on many similar super sportsters.

While the cylinder head looks almost the same from outside, it has been substantially modified and redesigned inside. The size of the valves has obviously changed as a result of the increase from a two to a four-valve unit. The two intake valves now measure 26.5 mm (1.04 in.) in diameter as opposed to the 34mm (1.34 in.) of the single intake valve on the former engine; exhaust valve diameter is now 23 mm (0.91 in.) on both valves instead of 28 mm (1.10 in.) on the single K100 exhaust valve. This modification and the central position of the spark plug reduced the fuels' octane requirement and enabled BMW's engineers to increase the compression ratio despite the better cylinder charge from 10.2:1 to 11:1 (95 ROM Euro super). Hence, the engine not only offers more power and extra torque, but is also more efficient and economical to run.

BMW's engineers consciously decided not to modify valve opening times just for the sake of increasing engine output at high running speeds. Accordingly, the four-valve power unit features the same relatively moderate, torque-orientated opening angle of 284 as its two-valve counterpart.

In the light of the positive experience gained with valve

Right: **Cylinder head details of K1 engine.**

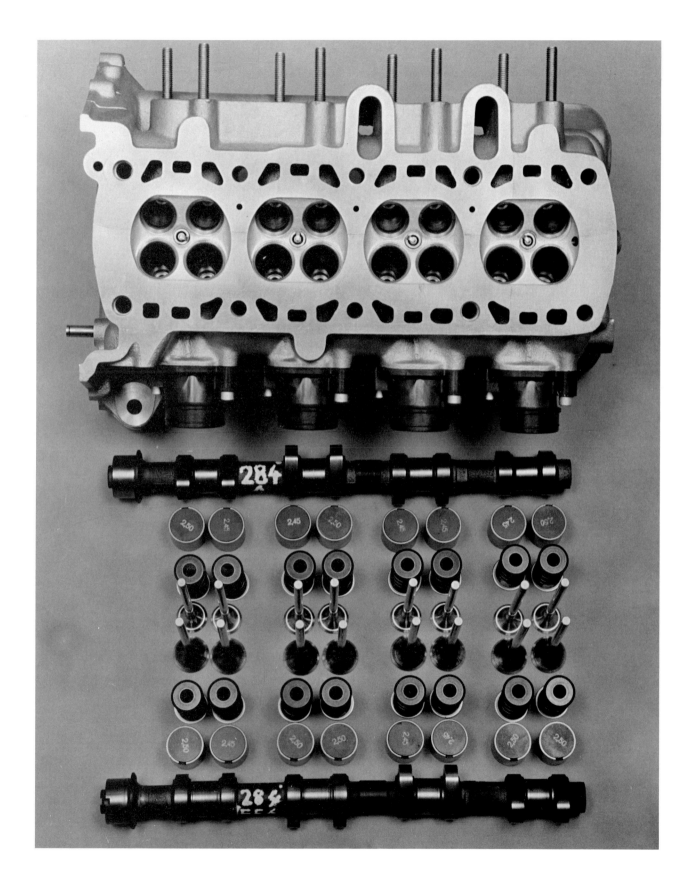

clearance remaining consistent over very long distances, BMW's engineers decided to modify the cup tappets of the four-valve power unit in order to reduce the mass of moving parts but achieve an even higher standard of reliability. As a result, the engine does not need the valve adjustment plates used on the two-valve power unit. If valve clearance has to be adjusted at all, which BMW claim is hardly ever the case with the new engine, all one has to do is choose the right tappet from a range of cup tappets with predetermined thicknesses.

The K1 features the same water-cooled light-alloy cylinder block as the K100 without any significant modifications. The relatively long-stroke of 70 mm (2.76 in.) compared with the bore of 67 mm (2.64 in.) intentionally chosen with this concept helps to keep the engine short and compact. Also providing very compact combustion chambers, this philosophy enhances the specific qualities of the K100 engine combining a high standard of fuel economy with an equally high standard of engine flexibility and running smoothness under part load unusual with a high-performance engine of this calibre.

A number of specific modifications and changes inside the engine of the K1 bear out BMW's quest for progress and the need to adjust to the extra power and performance of the engine. Applying new calculations based on the Finite Element Method, BMW's engineers succeeded in reducing the weight of the forged crankcase by 1.3kg (2.9lb). The same procedure was also applied to the connecting rods to optimise their weight, too. While this reduction of rotating masses in the engine serves to provide even better and smoother engine response, the use of lighter reciprocating components serves to minimise mass forces and, accordingly, reduce vibrations. This is also made possible by the new, slightly lighter pistons featuring a special labyrinth system around the piston rings to ensure that no oil is drawn in to the combustion chambers when the machine is parked on its side stand. Hence, the white smoke emitted by BMW inline engines when started again after parking, now becomes a thing of the past. Indeed, this improvement has now also been introduced on all K100 models from the 1989 model year.

The electronic engine management of the K1 features a significant innovation: While the ignition and fuel injection of the K100 had separate computer systems, the K1 boasts an integral Digital Motor Electronics "brain" as its already used in all of BMW's petrol car engines from the four-cylinder all the way to the V12.

Another new feature of the K1 is that it is no longer fitted with the butterfly-type air volume meter that inevitably causes an obstacle in the intake manifold. Instead, engine load is determined by the Digital Motor Electronics via a potentiometer on the throttle butterfly shaft transmitting data on the throttle butterfly opening angle to the engine management control unit. Sensors also determine engine speed, intake air temperature, coolant temperature and atmospheric air pressure (altitude) in order to establish the correct injection volume. This new, low-resistance intake system contributes 4 – 5 bhp to the extra power of the K1. Comparative measurements have also shown that it helps to reduce fuel consumption.

Left: **Complete engine assembly, with cam cover removed.**

Digital Motor Electronics also offers exemplary ease of service with the help of the integral defect memory allowing the diagnostic tester to retrieve defect information directly in the workshop. Failsafe functions ensure a higher standard of all-round dependability, keeping the engine running with limited power and performance should one of the components fail to operate.

The exhaust system of the K1 also presents striking innovations: The high-grade-steel exhaust pipe incorporates a silencer round in shape and not extending that far to the rear. Volume compensation is provided by an expansion chamber beneath the gearbox. Finally its appearance is greatly improved over the extremely ugly standard K100 component.

The actual power train of the K1 differs from that of the K100 by its various reinforcements and improvements to cope with the extra power, speed and performance. The only modification required in the gearbox was to give the fifth gear a "longer" transmission ratio, all other parts and components being quite sufficient for 100 bhp and 100 Nm (74 ft/lb). Maximum speed of the K1 is around 142 mph.

Applying the same general concept as the other K-models, the suspension and running gear of the K1 has been modified in every respect for the machine's superior performance. This is shown most clearly by the rear wheel featuring a single swinging arm as in the past, but now also incorporating BMW's unique Paralever patented worldwide and fitted on the R80 GS and R100 GS enduro models since Autumn 1987. The compensation of forces provided in this way offers significant advantages not only with long spring travel and on very rough, uneven terrain, but also when accelerating: It is claimed to eliminate the acceleration response typical of road machines with very powerful engines, even if they have relatively short spring travel.

The front forks are supplied by the same manufacturer that makes the forks of the BMW enduro: Italian specialist Marzocchi. Measuring 41.7 mm (1.64 in.), these boast particularly strong fork bridges and are designed for maximum torsional rigidity. The dampers chosen by BMW and a specialist supplier have a progressive response curve under compression most suitable for ensuring good road contact: Damper response remains at a minimum throughout the first 50 per cent of the total spring travel of 135 mm (5.31 in.), that is with the motorcycle fully laden but static, then becoming significantly harder on the remaining compression stroke until the dampers reach their hydraulic stop. The very sensitive response of the forks is enhanced by the teflon-coated sliding bushes for minimum friction and wear.

The new forks are fitted with Brembo brakes specially designed for the K1's superior performance. The twin brake discs feature spiral perforation to minimise weight and measure 305 mm (12.01 in.) in diameter and are 5 mm (0.20 in.) thick. Applying a technology used in racing, the brake discs move in axial direction on a follower bracket, providing "floating" suspension in cylinder-shaped supports. This racing type brake system is then rounded off by four-piston brake calipers. Interestingly, the pistons vary in diameter

(32 and 34 mm/1.26 and 1.34 in., respectively) in order to ensure absolutely equal brake pad wear on both sides.

By optimising the transmission ratio of the hydraulic system (piston diameter in the master cylinder versus piston diameter in the brake caliper), BMW have succeeded in substantially improving the response, accuracy and smoothness of the front-wheel brake.

The rear wheel of the K1 features the proven K100 brake system fitted with a thicker brake disc (5 instead of 4 mm/0.20 in. instead of 0.16 in.) in order to cope with higher temperatures and thermal loads.

The K1 (like all K100 models) is also available with ABS as an option, modified to the specific requirements of the K1 by BMW's development engineers.

Seeking to ensure optimum rear-wheel roadholding, the Paralever swinging arm is supported on the frame by a new, specially designed gas-pressure spring strut with 140 mm (5.51 in.) spring travel. The spring itself has a progressive-response curve and a travel-related damping effect. Depending on the load the motorcycle is carrying, the rider is easily able to adjust the readily accessible spring to four different positions.

Featuring new light-alloy wheels of three-spoke design and extra-wide rims with radial-ply tyres (120/70 VR-17 at the front,

Styling is best described as bold – note two tone seat, partial enclosure of front wheel and convenient (lockable) side carriers.

160/60 VR-18 at the rear), the K1 underlines its more sporting pretentions.

Since the demands made of the suspension and running gear increase overproportionally with increasing road speed (at a rate equal to road speed squared, according to the calculations of

As this photograph shows to advantage, fairing extends to give full enclosure underneath the engine.

BMW's test engineers), the frame of the K100 also had to be reinforced in order to meet the requirements of the K1. Hence, all tubes in the central load-bearing section are thicker and stronger. Stability has furthermore been enhanced by a 70 mm (2.76 in.) increase in wheelbase provided largely by the longer Paralever swinging arm and to a certain extent also by the modified wheel fork geometry. Showing a very high standard of directional stability in riding tests, the K1 has very short front-wheel caster of only 95 mm (3.74 in.) for optimum handling.

With the R100RS in 1976 and the K100 RS in 1983, BMW had already made history in aerodynamic motorcycle design. Now the K1 continues this heritage. Although the styling of the K1 is futuristic and bold (certainly by BMW standards) one of the main objectives in developing the new machine was to improve riding comfort and also effect a useful reduction in air drag. Hence, high priority in designing the fairing of the K1 was given to relaxed and fatigue-free touring at high speeds coupled with good protection from wind and weather. The need to meet these objectives required unconventional solutions – for example the front mudguard is quite different in its aerodynamic concept from the conventional assembly fitted to other K-series machines. One of the consequences of this new design is

that special air vents were required for effective cooling of the brakes.

The voluminous, wedge-shaped design of the front mudguard provides a completely enclosed, symmetrical fairing profile and, as a result, turbulence-free air flow along the full fairing, past the rider's legs and on to the end of the extra-wide rear section. The product of frontal area (A) and drag coefficient (cd) so vital to road performance is substantially lower than 0.4, thus allowing the K1 a higher maximum speed than would have otherwise been possible, given BMW's self imposed 100 bhp.

Seeking to achieve optimum riding stability in every respect, BMW's engineers spent weeks on refining the fairing in the wind tunnel, striving in particular to minimise front-wheel lift.

K1 even sports a totally new (and much prettier) silencer, than standard K100 series machines.

B M W

Futuristic location, Futuristic
motorcycle, BMW's four valve K1
Super Sports.

As with the other K-series machines, particular attention was also given to riding safety and ergonomics, the handlebars, seat and footrests being coordinated in their overall arrangement to provide the most suitable riding position. The rider's footrests, for example, were moved about 150 mm (5.91 in.) to the rear and 20 mm (0.79 in.) higher up. Seat height is 780 mm (30.71 in.), and the seat measures 700 mm (27.56 in.) in length. The rider also has the option to adjust the upholstered rear section by 30 mm (1.18 in.) to meet his personal requirements.

Knee-pads on the fairing are intended to absorb kinetic energy in the event of a head-on collision, helping the rider in conjunction with the pads on the inclined fuel tank to move up and "fly over" an obstacle – a configuration recommended by West German accident researchers.

And since BMW consider practical necessities remain important even with the most dynamic machine, the K1 comes with two small lockable stowage boxes (6 ltr/0.21 cu ft each) in the wide rear section. The rider can therefore take along odds and ends – but obviously not enjoy the use of panniers available to other K-series owners. BMW do however offer a tank bag as an "extra" for their Super Sportster.

A new central locking system combining the ignition and handlebar locking systems is another K1 innovation.

Through its radical appearance and more sporting riding position, the K1 clearly shows that it differs from BMW's previous models in that it does not seek to be the ideal touring machine in every respect. This greater orientation towards the super sports concept is also expressed by the fact that the K1 is not designed for fitting touring cases or panniers. Passenger comfort, however, has not been sacrificed to this sports concept, removal of the rear seat hump providing ample space and comfort behind the rider. And with its self imposed 100 bhp output, BMW have chosen to join the Super Sports arena through style and stamina, rather than the route taken by the Japanese of sheer power.

Only time will tell if the famous German marque has got its priorities right or not . . .

9

Road Tests

The K-Series is an awesome gamble for BMW's motorcycle division. Only time and the customer will show whether BMW were right to launch a major new product range at the height of a world recession in motorcycle sales.

K-Series Previewed October 1983 – Mick Walker

Hopefully, they will be successful; certainly they appear to have spent a lot of time and money in developing the new K-Series. For sixty years the flat twin concept has been the cornerstone of BMW's success. Will the inline 4 follow that tradition?

Its strength lies in three main areas and I believe that the K-Series will be a winner for BMW. Firstly – power without weight; although water-cooled the K-Series machines will be the lightest in their class, a welcome change from 'more complex means heavier'. Secondly – price; the standard K100 costs £3290 (including taxes) and BMW seem determined to be winners in the price war, currently being fought by manufacturers and retailers. Finally – the engine; this appears to be one of the most advanced ever conceived for motorcycle use, a unit which should ensure BMW success in the future.

First reports indicate that the horizontal straight 4 provides plenty of *power* and *torque;* this plus a low centre of gravity and its lightness in relation to the power available should mean that the K100 is a real rider's bike. Shaft drive eliminates the bogey of the superbike – the drive chain. Unlike many big bore multis, the K100 engine is easy to get at and work on – an important factor with ever rising service costs.

The dry weight of the K100 is 474lbs. The K100RS, which will be available at the end of the year, will be 22lbs heavier. The K100RT tourer, which will be launched in the spring of '84, will tip the scales at 504.9lbs but this includes full touring equipment.

All housing components and the cylinder head of the 998cc flat four (70mm stroke x 67mm bore) are made of a light alloy. The crankcase and cylinder head cover are mounted on rubber elements to reduce noise. To increase wear resistance, the cylinder barrels are lined with nickel-silicon carbide. The two overhead camshafts are supported at 5 points. A hydraulic tensioner makes for a maintenance-free timing chain. The water and oil pumps are driven directly via the input shaft and alternator. An electronically controlled fuel injection system, similar to that used in BMW cars, is

K100 Launch
First example of the big gamble, the K100 launched in October 1983.

installed with a fuel supply shut off. The liquid cooling system is thermostatically controlled by a dual circuit pump drive.

The electrical circuit comprises a 460-watt alternator with a fully integrated electronic regulator. The powerful 55/60 watt headlight receives power from a 12v 24amp hour battery. The instrument cluster features an electronic speedo and rev counter, plus other gadgetry normally found on machines in this price range.

A forged alloy flywheel (with asbestos free pads) makes the single plate clutch a far superior item to that used on earlier BMWs.

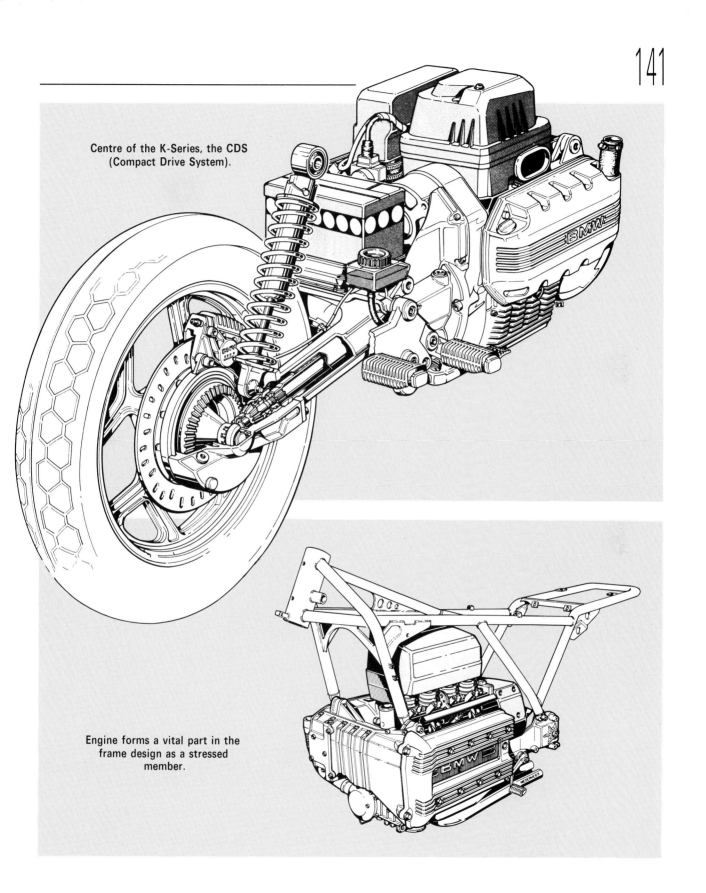

Centre of the K-Series, the CDS (Compact Drive System).

Engine forms a vital part in the frame design as a stressed member.

The gearbox is flange-mounted, 5 speed with integrated shock absorber and weight reducing aluminium components.

The quoted power output is 90bhp at 8000rpm. Compression ratio 10.2 to 1. Maximum torque 63.7lbs ft at 6000rpm. BMW claim a maximum speed of 133mph for their K-Series bikes.

Engine support is a vital part of the frame design with a single rear shock on the offside of the forged alloy swinging arm. The massive front forks have a tube diameter of 41.4mm and are manufactured by BMW. Low profile high speed tubeless tyres are standard (100/90 V18 front and 130/90 V17 rear) and these are fitted to 8 spoke cast alloy wheels.

Brembo calipers are used together with special slotted steel discs. Semi-metallic pads mean superior braking in both wet and dry weather conditions. The disc diameter of all three is 285mm.

To sum up, in my opinion BMW has taken a gamble but a calculated one. Their brochure states 'There are flashier motorcycles, but these are designed to appeal to the flashier biker rather than the true enthusiast'.

K100RT Tested October 1984 – Mick Walker

Never before has a European motorcycle had such press coverage as the new BMW K100-Series when it was launched. The standard version appeared in October 1983, to be followed shortly afterwards by the RS with sport fairing and finally the top of the line, the fully dressed K100RT tourer, arrived this summer.

When I put the original K100 design concept under the microscope in October 1983, I concluded that BMW had created a machine to carry the marque into the future and, with the launch price of £3290, it was a bargain buy.

Well, how does this statement stand up one year on, now that all three versions are in the showrooms? For a start, there is no doubt the new in-line 4 cylinder has been a sales success for BMW – certainly in Britain – and has assisted the importers to outmanoeuvre their rivals in actually increasing sales when others were seeing dramatic reductions. This is in no small part due to the effort put in by the German company in the development of the design and the publicity which it has aroused in the popular press.

Most K100 tests have dealt in great detail with the technical side of the newcomer, so this RT test is more about what it is like to ride and how it performs in service. When I collected the K100RT from BMW's Bracknell headquarters I was instantly impressed by the superb level of finish, even by BMW's standards. With a complete absence of bright chrome plate, here is a bike which cannot be labelled flashy or garish but is nonetheless crowd-pulling.

In my book the RT is a much more noticeable bike than the standard K100 and, to a lesser extent, the RS sportster. This is entirely due to its touring stance, which revolves around the massive fairing and panniers. These succeed in transforming the whole bike, giving it the feel and look of almost, dare I say it, a two-wheeled car.

For one thing, the fairing distances the rider from the tarmac like no other motorcycle I have ever ridden. The level of safety features and warning devices all add to this impression.

There were several other surprises in store during the miles ahead, some of the RT's own making, some heightened by the last bike I had ridden, the flat twin BMW R80G/S trail bike.

This bike, the K100RT, is totally different; it is like comparing an open Morgan Plus 4 with a Daimler. The RT exudes luxury, comfort, quality, plus excellent equipment and the solidness of a Daimler. The G/S is by comparison raw and basic although still with more than a touch of class, but pure fun – just like a Morgan.

K100RT Test

In its premier role, that of long-distance touring – usually with a pillion passenger.

RT is a machine to make full use of the K100's high engine torque which, allied to weather protection, riding stance and carrying capacity, have created a unique combination.

However, the RT is what a touring motorcycle is really all about. So forget anything sporting, the rest of this test features motorcycling with a relaxed, touring flavour. If one accepts this principle, the K100RT emerges as an excellent bike. But be warned! If you want anything else, look for another model.

After having the large number of controls and equipment explained to me by Chris Pereira of BMW GB, I set off to Cambridgeshire via the M4 and A1. Here came the first surprise; at 50mph I honestly thought that there were more gears in the box for, although the tacho only read 3000rpm, the engine seemed to be working hard and wanting another gear, but I was already in top. What I was soon to discover is that, in reality, once it passes 50mph the motor will run up like a turbine to 110mph at which, if anything, it seems less stressed than at 50mph.

Stated maximum is 134mph, but this is a bit pointless as it is at speeds from 60mph to 110mph where the RT's comfortable cruising gait reveals itself, whilst at the other end it is possible to drop down to 20mph (still in top) and actually pull away with no transmission snatch whatsoever. For a multi-cylinder unit this is unbelievable, but true. With such a flexible engine in a pure touring machine, why feature a 5-speed gearbox? Certainly this is one bike which only needs three speeds, so why not offer an automatic option? Not with a Guzzi V100 type torque converter, but the auto transmission found in larger cars: 1st, 2nd, drive and park. Currently, an RT rider familiar with other large capacity modern bikes has to learn to ride it without constantly cog-swapping once top is reached.

One is not aware of the BMW's weight and size until stationary, then its bulk is evident when attempting to manoeuvre it. Operating the centre stand is more difficult than I expected, but an excellent prop stand helps. One other point to watch: when coming to a halt and putting a foot down to support the bike, it is very easy to catch your shin on the rear section of the side fairing; this is more noticeable when carrying a pillion passenger.

There are many safety features on the machine including various warning lights, the most unusual of which is one which stays on until *both* brake light switches have been activated for the first time. I found the amber and red fuel warning lights tiresome with the amber coming on intermittently after approximately 130 miles, followed at around 150 by the red as well. With a tank capacity of almost 5 gallons and a consumption which averages around 50mpg, this seems rather overdone. A couple of very useful additions were the quartz clock and digital gear indicator.

One of the very few items in the control layout to have survived from the flat twin models is the choke lever. I praised this on the R65LS test and I praise it again. The fuel-injected K100 motor is very good and the choke lever can be set back to zero within a few seconds. I later discovered that because of the fuel injection, the

Bottom section of fairing provides leg and foot protection from the elements unmatched by any other K-Series bike.

choke is not needed except in the most extreme of winter conditions. The switchgear took some getting used to, but once it becomes familiar there are no problems. The horn button has to be watched, as pressing it by mistake makes you very unpopular as the twin horns are the loudest I have ever heard on a bike and are guaranteed to make offenders jump and take notice even in the fast lane on motorways. The H4 Bosch headlight is also top class, extra bright and penetrating. The fairing provides the kind of protection many riders would not have dreamt possible a few years ago and there is a distinct reduction in the level of wind noise. The only disadvantage with the fairing is when passing heavy vehicles – like buses or trucks – on motorways and riding in gale force conditions when extra care and attention is called for. Incidentally, it does not afford pillion passengers the same level of protection. The panniers seemed inferior to those fitted to the flat twins – they were constructed from a plastic material and allowed water in even when stationary. Another water culprit was the filler cap. This cap, while not allowing water to actually drip straight into the tank, collects water around the inner rim so one has to be careful when opening the cap after anything more than a light shower.

Majestic appearance of RT is visible in this photograph.

As a tourer the RT's suspension, roadholding and braking are without reproach; the exception is its tendency to drop into slow corners a shade too easily. The Michelin tyres gave every confidence in both wet and dry conditions.

Ride and comfort are fully in keeping with the BMW tradition, but pillion passengers voiced their dissatisfaction about the recessed grab handles, preferring something easier to 'grab'. A sharp edge at the front of the saddle was pointed out to me by a K100 owner but, although I could detect this on the test bike, it never gave me any problems. The seat itself is lockable and when opened revealed a compartment hidden in the seat tail. This contains a first aid kit, various literature and a comprehensive tool roll. To make life easier, the seat is hinged – a nice touch.

Although the RT's instrument console resembles an airliner's flight deck, the rest of the bike continues the traditional simple BMW approach. This is much appreciated when it comes to servicing or working on the bike and even applied to the suspension, which is the BMW 'Monolever' alloy swinging arm, supported by a single suspension unit with only three positions.

Please BMW, even though you are now making an ultra smooth, watercooled, fuel injected, four cylinder technical masterpiece, do not attempt to take on your Japanese competitors at their own game – that of who can cram in the most technical features on one motorcycle. At present the K100RT offers the advantages of both worlds, a smooth effortless power delivery with the promise that your new purchase will not be obsolete next year.

If you are serious about touring then consider the BMW K100RT, but take a test ride first to convince yourself that you want a complete tourer and nothing else. At £4,490 the RT is not cheap, but nevertheless is very competitive against other fully-dressed large capacity touring mounts from Japan or America.

K100RS Tested March 1985 – Mick Walker

When testing the K100RT I had been impressed with many aspects of the machine, especially its smoothness and the tremendous amount of torque available. In fact, I found that it was possible to drop down to 20mph and still pull away smoothly, experiencing no transmission snatch whatsoever, which was remarkable for a multi-cylinder unit. My main grouse was about the fairing which, although giving a high degree of protection, distanced the rider from the road – more like driving a car than riding a bike.

This was uppermost in my thoughts when I set off on the K100RS. However, instead of that 'two wheel car' feeling experienced on the RT, I felt completely at ease on the RS. On this version the fairing combined with the narrow handlebars gave an almost perfect riding stance. Although the RS uses the same frame, suspension and engine assembly as its touring stablemate, BMW have managed to create two entirely different machines. Whether the RS was silently moving through London traffic or cruising at the legal limit on a motorway, it managed both with consummate ease.

The RS is certainly a modern multi which does everything, but it

still retains three very important qualities: engine flexibility, a design that will not be obsolete next year and it is eminently easy to live with. To my mind, these features account for BMW's success with the K-Series and the RS in particular.

I cannot say that I am over-excited by the styling, but once on the road the bike speaks for itself. Although many of us have bought a new motorcycle because of its up-to-the-minute styling, I doubt that anyone would fall into that trap with the K100RS. The popular press have in fact labelled the K100 Series *The Flying Brick.*

Unlike the K100RT, which is very much a touring only bike, the RS is a machine that any type of rider would appreciate. Although, like any BMW, it is expensive, the number of roles it successfully fulfils makes it extremely good value.

As far as performance is concerned, the factory quote a maximum speed of 137mph which is some 4 miles an hour faster than either the standard K100 or the fully-faired RT. In many ways, as most experienced riders will appreciate, what happens above 100mph is purely of academic value unless you are going in for

K100RS Test

K100RS – a machine which transformed the previously lacklustre K100 into a civilised sportster with the addition of a fairing and very little else.

production road racing. Of greater importance is what happens when you are in top gear at 55mph, climbing a hill two up, or overtaking; here the flexibility of the K100 engine unit shows its real forte – torque. In fact, I feel that the BMW brochure sums up the performance very succinctly: 'up to well over 6000rpm, the K-Series engine produces more power to the back wheel than nominally more powerful machines of greater capacity'.

987cc four-cylinder engine pulls like a train from 20mph up to a near 140mph maximum.

At 496lbs dry the K100RS is no lightweight, but the only time I noticed its weight was when turning in a restricted area. However, it is easy to be caught off balance and run the risk of dropping it and a smaller rider than I (I am 5ft 10ins) could have problems. The seat height certainly does not help, being almost 32 inches high and this is without doubt one area which scores minus points.

Whilst testing the RS my thoughts went back to a long distance endurance race I had watched last year. Competing in the event were a couple of K100RS and their only visible disadvantage was that their rear wheels tended to lock up under the heavy braking conditions required to take the chicane. However, on the road I did not experience this problem, so am fairly happy to say that under normal conditions, wet or dry, the stainless steel discs and Brembo calipers can cope with most eventualities. I also found that the handling was more than adequate for anything normal road use could throw at it.

The fairing offers a level of protection which is far greater than its size suggests and the mirrors/indicators form a very effective wind barrier for the rider's hands. The only really unprotected parts of the body are one's legs and feet, especially the latter which are completely exposed to the elements.

Both stands operate relatively easily, once you have got used to the lifting handle provided to assist with the centre stand action – without it you would probably suffer a hernia.

This time round I found the switchgear easy to live with, but this was because I had encountered the same layout on the RT. However, I must admit that this does tend to confirm a theory I have held for some time:- although we all accept that Japanese switchgear is the best, it might just be because the majority of bikes we test are Japanese.

If the mood takes you, the K100RS is well able to perform as a credible tourer. A road test bike away from it all, posing near a Scottish loch.

The only thing which I would seriously consider changing if I owned the K100RS would be the exhaust. Not because I wish to make a racket, but because its looks and bulk just do not match up with the bike's image. However, I was lucky enough to test two bikes, the completely standard model and one fitted with a German performance exhaust system which, although not much noisier, produced a lovely sound. The replacement exhaust was certainly a better looking item and improved the performance of the machine – the increased performance is claimed to be an extra 2bhp at the rear wheel. I must say that I was very impressed with this system, although at £175 plus VAT it is not cheap.

Another variation of the RS theme offered by several dealers is a 'Motorsport' version – this was prior to the factory's limited edition machine. The machine is finished in white and decked out with red and blue stripes which give a more aggressive and sporting line. Whereas the K100RS in its more familiar dark metallic blue or silver guise is very much the tasteful Teutonic masterpiece.

Having tested the BMW K100RS, I am no longer surprised that there are so many around, even though the current asking price is now £4650, and would agree that they do really deserve the title of the 'world's most civilised superbike'.

K75C Tested October 1985 – Mick Walker

The K75C has been both praised and slated by the road testers of the popular press, so I was very curious to find out what it would really be like in the metal. Luckily, we always have BMWs out on test for at least a couple of weeks which is time enough to get a real impression of the bike and, frankly, I was agreeably surprised.

Okay, the new three cylinder K75C obviously cannot compete with the latest super sportsters from Japan in the performance stakes, but who cares? Here is a touring bike with enough sporting performance to satisfy most experienced road riders. In my opinion, the K75C is in many ways more fun to ride than the K100 *and* has the bonus of being a smoother machine. It also encourages a more sporting riding style than the four-cylinder motor it is derived from – you have only to snick down a gear (or two!) and the K75C actually growls, almost like a civilised Trident or Rocket-3!

Perhaps one of the reasons why the K75C has upset some journalists is that it is so good at being a totally practical everyday, go-anywhere machine. There is not even a hint of the uncivilised; right from the moment you start the motor – first time, every time – to when you coast almost silently to a halt at the end of a journey, however long. While stationary, I found the K75C more manageable than its four-cylinder brother and, when out on the road, the handling seems much lighter. One K-Series complaint has not been rectified, however, namely the height of the seat and I further contend that the K75C's upholstery is actually harder than the K100's!

The only real flaw in the K75C's role as the ideal sports-tourer is that BMW have for once followed fashion rather than function and fitted a fairing which leaves the hands almost totally exposed. In my view this limits the bike's (or rather the rider's) ability to cover the long distances that it is so manifestly capable of doing.

This is a shame as I am sure most potential K75C owners are real riders and not poseurs.

For much of the K75 read K100 but, besides the engineering legacy and the cosmetic differences, what else has changed? Well, for a start the engine capacity is three quarters that of the original and this makes sense not only from the point of view of development, but also in terms of spare parts supply. As already mentioned, the three is smoother than the four; in fact BMW claim that it is the smoothest 750 in the world.

Besides the fact of 'chopping off' one of the K100's cylinders, BMW engineers decided to reprofile the combustion chamber when they developed the K75. A more hemispherical shape allows a higher compression ratio of 11:1 instead of 10.2:1. The piston design is also new for the K75, but it shares con-rods with the K100. The result is a claimed output of 75bhp for the new engine as compared with 90bhp for the K100 and this improved hp/litre ratio means that both power/rpm and torque figures are significantly higher. Maximum output is now at 8500rpm compared to 8000 for the K100 and the K75 develops 68Nm (50ft lb) of torque at 6750rpm as against 86Nm (63ft lb) at 6000rpm for the K100.

The K-Series engines are closely related in terms of their auxiliary units. In both cases the ignition is contact-free and computer controlled. The only special feature of the K75 in this context is the asymmetric arrangement of the two induction points on the rotor at 120 degrees and 240 degrees crankshaft angle. The ignition of the three-cylinder engine therefore requires two pulses for cylinders one and three since the control pulse of the second cylinder is determined directly in the computer on the basis of this data.

The fully electronic ignition of the K75 also acts as a speed governor by retarding the ignition advance from 8777rpm. This effect is enhanced from 8905rpm by switching off the fuel injection.

K75C Test

Surprise packet. When the K75C three-cylinder was launched, testers were surprised by the smooth, revvy nature of its 740cc engine.

Main criticism centred round an over-soft suspension and the over-small, handlebar mounted fairing which gave only very limited protection.

The Bosch LE-Jetronic electronic fuel injection with its air-volume metering by means of a butterfly is basically the same as the K100's. The three injection jets inject fuel simultaneously every crankshaft rotation, the volume being determined by the digital control unit in accordance with the engine output curve. This depends on engine speed, the position of the air-volume meter and the injection period. In coasting, cut-off operates at engine speeds down to 2000rpm, a starter repeat lock being activated from a speed of 711rpm.

At first sight the power transmission of the K75 looks to be exactly like that of the K100 – indeed all five gears have the same number of teeth and the same ratios.

In fact, BMW engineers felt it only necessary to modify the final drive by choosing a shorter transmission ratio. However, since the three-cylinder layout presents a completely different situation as regards balance of the masses, it was not sufficient to simply compensate the free mass momentum by adding counterweights to the drive shaft. In addition, the power transmission of the K75 must tally with the larger firing gaps and the reduced uniformity of the triple-pot layout. There is therefore a rigid connection between the drive shaft and the clutch, but without any dampers in between. This made it possible to use a somewhat lighter clutch, borrowed – in a modified form – from the R80.

Three cylinders also required a redesigned exhaust system. The shape of the silencer has also changed – this, say BMW, is a discreet indication of the number of cylinders; whilst the K100 has a square silencer, the one fitted to the K75 has three 'rounded' sides to it – what else? Still in stainless steel, though.

The K75 (as tested) had a 200mm drum brake at the rear, whereas the more sporting K75S features a rear disc. I personally do not feel the need for a rear disc and I am sure many everyday riders will appreciate the drum. My only complaint with an otherwise perfect braking system was that the brakes squeal at low speeds – a problem which I have experienced with most BMWs I have tested over the last couple of years. The K75, like the K100, has dual discs at the front, each of 285mm diameter, and Italian Brembo calipers.

Test K75C outside Mick Walker's Wisbech home.

As on the R80 (but not on the K100) the two fork tubes are connected by a brace. With a diameter of 41.4mm, the stanchions fitted to the K-Series must be some of the strongest fitted to any production motorcycle.

B M W

K75C makes an excellent sports/tourer and is well-liked by passengers.

BMW has not been tempted by the fashion for 16-inch wheels and, although I cannot say that the K75s (or the K100s, for that matter) are beautiful-looking motorcycles, they do offer a blend of quality and practical performance that is hard to beat.

I have left performance and price to the last, but for different reasons. I am convinced that a BMW customer is not especially concerned if his machine will do 120 or 160mph and, to be honest, unlike some journalists I see no point in trying to extract the last ounce of performance from a machine anyway . . . what owner in his right mind honestly would? However, the factory claim a maximum speed of 124mph for the K75C.

Price is another matter. With only £137 separating the K75 from the K100, the new machine is certainly not going to sell because it is cheaper. So, the burning question must be – is it good, or even better than the K100? Personally I preferred the K75. It is smoother, sportier, handles more easily and is more economical in terms of consumption, insurance and tyres. But perhaps more important than all of these, it has more character. Unfortunately I fear that too many potential buyers will ultimately pick the K100 because it has more cubes – which is a pity. Certainly as far as I am concerned, the K75 rates as one of the best bikes I have ever ridden.

K75S/100RS Comparison. Tested June & July 1986 – Mick Walker

With the exception of market leaders Honda, the German company BMW is currently the most widely known motorcycle marque inside *and* outside the two wheel world.

This is because both companies have, over the last few years, made great efforts promoting their respective brands. The fruits of this have benefited both, but in differing ways. Honda is now viewed very much as the Ford of the motorcycle industry, whilst BMW have strengthened their hold on the top end, the prestige sector.

For some sixty years the German company had been associated with the flat twin but, in late 1983, all this changed with the introduction of the first of the new K-Series, a four-cylinder based around what BMW labelled the Compact Drive System. Then late last year an extension of the original, three-cylinder triple.

When a new BMW is launched, both the parent company in Germany and our own British importers in Bracknell go about the whole business in a highly professional *and* successful manner. Witness their very latest, the K75S Sportster. Not content with a simple, soulless mail-shot, BMW organised a real launch with the superb and traffic-free west coast of Scotland as a magnificent backdrop for a few lucky members of the press. Not only did a gleaming line of the brand new K75S triples greet our eyes, but there was a chance to test most of the '86 range to boot.

Based near Aberfoyle, the original plan was for all of us to do around 500 miles over a couple of days and then ride a K75S back south, covering more miles over the following two weeks before returning the machine to BMW's Bracknell headquarters. However, I decided to take this a stage further to produce an in-depth comparison test between the newcomer and the well-established

K100RS, including the limited-edition Motorsport model. Being able to step straight off one model on to another was a great advantage, as was the ability to ride several different machines of the same type, ranging from brand new to relatively high mileage examples.

Previously when testing earlier K100s, I had been generally impressed but with certain provisos, namely mid-range vibration and a couple of problems caused by water getting into the fuel via the tank cap and ditto for the panniers when parked on the side stand.

In their press handout BMW says that the introduction of the K75S completes the K-Series range; if so, what about the rumoured K75RT? Taking BMW at its word, there are now five K-Series models. Two use the three-cylinder 750 engine and three the four-cylinder 1000. With four of the conventional flat twins in the 650/800 category, the company now have a comprehensive range of bikes to cater for – dare I say it – the older more experienced rider than ever before. Having said that, it is worth stating without hesitation that of all of these the new K75S is the most sporting. This may seem a strange statement. given that its engine is to an identical state of tune as the touring C model. The difference lies in its running gear. The wind tunnel–designed fairing adds another 6mph to maximum speed, even though it is not as comprehensive as the one fitted to the K100RS.

Another difference to the C is the use of a rear disc brake (straight off the K100RS) instead of the previous drum. But the major change lies in the suspension. The front fork spring travel has been reduced to 135mm and two springs in each fork leg provide a double progressive rate. Entirely new is the damping system. The damper is fitted only in the left fork leg. BMW claims this allows better oil flow behaviour and finer tuning. The rear mono-shock has also been revised internally to provide better sensitivity.

Otherwise the S retains the same characteristics as the K75C. This means that although on paper the engine produces 83% of its maximum torque at a low 2500rpm – whilst the figure for the K100RS is only marginally different at 85% – this does not reveal any noticeable difference where it counts, on the open road. Here the smaller unit is more akin to a Japanese-inspired design with its taste for revs, whereas its larger four-cylinder brother is quite happy to remain in top for the majority of any journey. This is not to say that the K75S is not tractable, just that it thrives when driven hard through the gears. As a point of interest, the K100RS is quite happy for top to be engaged at 20mph – whilst below 30mph on the K75S you are wasting your time. A feature of riding the K100RS after the triple is that for the first few miles you are constantly trying to change into top when you are already there, such is the torque-bound nature of the four cylinder unit compared to the much freer revving three.

At anything below 80mph I preferred the smaller bike. This was because below this speed the engine was dead smooth, whilst the K100RS has quite a bad patch of the vibes at around 3500rpm (between 53-59mph). Strangely, above 80mph I found the larger engine came into its own and was actually *smoother* than the triple which seemed to suffer a slight amount of vibration just above this

K75S/K100RS Comparison Test

K75S – most sporting of the Ks.

figure, particularly when new (up to 1000 miles). It is worth noting that on machines with more than 2500 miles the K100RS also became smoother, but never lost its roughness in the same way.

With 75bhp (90bhp on K100RS) the K75S not only lacks the torque of the larger unit, but also suffers as a pure motorway bike where the 1000 scores well. But on minor roads, city work or hard riding over anything other than dead smooth surfaces, the K75S is definitely superior. Unlike the C version, the S also scores against its bigger brother in price – it is £755 cheaper at £4131. It is also some 14kg (32lb) lighter but, regrettably, the tall seat height is the same.

Gearbox action on both bikes is truly superb – as good as anything with chain drive, but without the mess. (It should be noted

K100RS – that fairing not only gives superior protection from the elements, but gives its rider a real sense of security.

that owners of new K-Series bikes may find their box crunchy. This tends to improve greatly between 600-2000 miles as the gearbox needs running in). The clutch is not quite as slick as the best of the Japs, but light years ahead of that on many big-bore Italian machines. Conversely, the brakes, even though equipped with Brembo calipers, did not match those found on most Italians equipped with triple Brembos. However, in their favour BMW stainless steel discs did not rust and were exceptionally safe to use, only blotting their copybook with the front units needing careful watching below 5mph to avoid grabbing.

Compared to the K75S, the fairing on the K100RS is one of the best features of the whole machine. Not only does it offer superior protection from the elements, but gives its rider a real sense of security. In addition, the mirrors serve a real function – during a cloud burst my hands remained completely dry whilst travelling along the M11 motorway in Essex, amazing but true. The fairing on the K75S is better than it looks, offering some protection against wind buffeting, but failing to add the security dimension of the larger machine's streamlining.

Another failing of the K75S is the power of its horn – or rather lack of it – compared to the penetrating note emitted from the twin units fitted to the K100RS.

Both Ks use stainless steel exhaust systems, ugly but effective. Of the two, the unit fitted to the K75S has the best appearance, but against this the pipes on the smaller engine end up an angry shade of blue, whereas those on the K100RS remained a straw colour on all the machines I used – and saw – during the test period. I also noticed, as on the K75C tested last year, that the K75S would on occasion pop back on the overrun, something I have never experienced on any of the K100s. This I later discovered is due to incorrect CO adjustment.

A feature of both engines, however, is that when parked on the side stand for more than a few minutes, a plume of white smoke is emitted for the first few seconds after starting the engine. This also happens to a lesser extent when left on the centre stand overnight. Even so, throughout the test period none of the machines used any oil!

Previous complaints of leaky fuel caps and the highly annoying dual fuel warning lights have been rectified. The speedo is still prone to misting up in wet weather, however. The lifting handle for the centre stand is much appreciated, although the mousetrap action of the currently fitted side stand is not. The latter can easily catch the unwary off balance.

Most of the K-Series machines tested had BMW touring panniers fitted. Not only do these blend well with the lines of the machine, unlike most others, but they are completely safe even at maximum speed. Not so long ago manufacturers were warning riders with panniers fitted not to exceed 70mph. BMW deserves praise here.

On tyres, I noticed that most of my fellow journalists tended to pick machines with any make of tyre except Continental. As I was one of the last to collect a K75S when returning to England, I found myself with a machine fitted with a pair of these 'unwanted' tyres. Actually, I was pleasantly surprised and, although I did not go round Snetterton or Brands Hatch with them, I found the Continentals perfectly suitable for everyday use, providing grip in both wet and dry conditions. In fact, on one K100RS fitted with Pirelli tyres, these tended to *lose* adhesion at the front in slippery conditions.

Tyre wear seems a good feature on the K-Series. A friend of mine has done over 10,000 miles and is still on his original *rear* tyre!

At first glance – and feel – there is not much to give the rider or passenger any real hope of comfort from the relatively hard saddle. But, as the miles unwind, you suddenly realise that although firm that seat is really good. Many seats give the initial impression of being comfortable and turn out just the reverse. With the K-Series sportsters, it is just the opposite.

I also had the chance to sample the top of the line K100RS Motorsport. This caters for someone wanting a more aggressive and exclusive machine than the standard model. For an extra £192 the owner gets one of only 120 machines imported. Finish is in an attractive metallic pearl white, decked out in BMW Motorsport decals, while the windscreen, engine block and wheel rims are in black. Front suspension is straight off the K75S, with Pirelli Radial tyres as standard. Performance is identical to the standard model, but handling improved over uneven surfaces.

Finish of the normal K100RS and K75S is in a range of rather reserved metallic shades including dark blue, red gunmetal grey and silver. I also rode a K100RS in all black – a most attractive scheme which suited the BMW well.

The K75 triple has, I feel, been clearly aimed at those who would never have previously considered one of the German bikes and should find favour with riders weaned on Japanese multis, or those wanting to ride harder than BMW's touring image would previously allow. Meanwhile, the K100RS caters for those wanting to go slow *or* fast, but either way concentrating on major A-roads or motorways because under this type of going the machine is at its best. In addition, anyone brought up on British or European machinery will find its torquey power to their liking and will more easily accept its vibration.

Both machines would be unlikely to top any conventional performance rating in their respective classes but, if taken *overall,* the picture is very different. Here I feel is the secret of BMW's present level of success, combined with the fact that neither will be obsolete either next year, or the year after. These features will, I am sure, mean that there will be even more converts to the BMW camp in the future. I know that at the end of the six weeks and 5000 miles I was genuinely sorry to end the relationship.

How often is it possible to test a manufacturer's complete range of machines on the same day, under the same conditions? Recently I was lucky enough to ride the entire BMW fleet around Donington Park race circuit. The man responsible for this was Jim Blanchard of South Humberside solus BMW specialist, Harvey's. Jim is an old friend and is the brother of former racing star John Blanchard whom many readers will remember for his exploits aboard a variety of machinery in the 1960s and later as team manager for the German Münch factory in the early 1970s.

Arriving at Donington at around 9.30 on a dry but overcast day, I wondered if the weather would hold long enough for some six hours of concentrated riding which was was to follow but, for once in a dismally wet summer, it remained dry *almost* all day.

Strangely, the first bike I took around the Donington swervery, a K75C, was also to prove one of my favourites of the day. Afterwards I returned several times to this bike to make sure – and yes, it really

1987 BMW Range Tested July 1987 – Mick Walker

was an excellent combination of smoothness, sufficient performance, easy handling and with no nasty surprises for its rider. Also, around Donington's relatively smooth surface the oversoft suspension I had noticed on our road test bike (*MCE* Jan/Feb '86) was not a problem, in fact it was not even noticeable.

Next came the standard K100. This is a machine I had never ridden, although I was well-versed with the four cylinder power unit, having tested both the RT tourer and the RS sportster. Unlike its smaller three-cylinder brother, the one litre model has even more torque; in fact, in my opinion it may be *too* much, giving an almost muscle-bound feel to its power delivery in top gear between 40-60mph. It is quite possible to drop down to 20mph in top and accelerate smoothly away right up to its maximum of around 130mph. But compared with the RS and RT, the lack of a fairing really makes itself felt above 80mph – as evidenced by an overdose of wind buffeting. It was entirely possible to ride any of the K100 models around Donington without the need of ever changing down from top; the full GP circuit with its connecting loop was not used.

The extra weight and bulk of the four made itself felt over the K75, as did the extra harshness of power delivery.

I then took out a fully-faired K100LT, which is a deluxe version of the similarly equipped RT model. As on the road test example I had a couple of years back, the most noticeable feature was that huge fairing – divorcing as it does the rider from the normal close working relationship with the unwinding road. Two years on, I am no nearer to accepting that, in riding-for-fun terms, this fairing is nothing more than a bucket of water is to a red blooded young lover – quite simply, it removed in one throw all the essential 'one-ness' between rider and his machine. OK, it is fine for weather protection and long distance motorway cruising but removes in the process the last vestiges of a sports riding stance.

Although in pure weight terms not greatly different from the other K100s, the LT – and RT for that matter – give the impression of being far less manoeuvrable.

The K100RS is, in my opinion, the best of the fours, making for a good sports tourer which is easy to live with. Contrasting with its touring stablemate, the fairing on the RS is a real boon – just big enough to offer a good level of protection but small enough not to give the rider problems as described above. The only real faults are that ugly slab-sided black silencer, an over-tall seat height (the same on all K-series bikes) and an engine which could do with being smoother and carrying a shade higher gearing.

The cheapest K-Series model is the unfaired K75. This was debuted at the Cologne show in September '86 and, although available from earlier this year in Britain, has not really been pushed by BMW. This is strange because not only is it within reach of many more prospective owners, but in appearance it is quite different to the other models. Most striking is the colour of its seat – bright orange/red – unusual for the normally staid BMW image (more like Honda's CB350S). The K75 is available in only one colour scheme – black, with that red seat and red pin-striping. Several parts such as the large 170mm Bosch H4 headlight, carrier at the rear of the seat and exhaust guard are, unlike the other models in the range, finished in sparkling chrome. But why on a machine which now costs over £4,000 is an untidy exposed area left around the ignition units, which to make matters worse, sport garish *red* plug leads!

The balance of the triple range is made up by the sporting S variant. This has firmer springing than the other machines – both threes and fours – and is all the much better for it if one intends riding in a truly sporting manner. The fairing is not as comprehensive as the K100RS, but is more effective in wet conditions than one might imagine at first glance.

There is also a limited edition S Special – commonly nicknamed the SS – in either black or silver with black wheels and engine, the swinging arm and rear hub in black as well on the silver bike.

Certainly around Donington the K75S/SS was the nicest of any K-Series models tried. The engine is in the same state of tune for all the K75 models (and for that matter on the respective fours) – so smoothness is just as good with the streamlining working well at high speeds, not only to protect the rider from the gale, but also offering a considerable increase in top end performance.

Then came the classic boxers – how would they fare in relation to the new K-Series? We have all read the headlines in *MCN* regarding the return 'by demand' of the much-lamented R100RS.

Standard K75 suffered at Donington Park compared to C and S versions through lack of a fairing at higher speeds.

For a start it must be remembered that the reborn R100RS is rather a larger capacity R80 monoshock with an RS fairing than the real thing. It is also – at £5,000 – mighty expensive. Regardless of the rose-tinted 'I love boxers' brigade, I feel that it is not only too expensive, but it is not as good either as the K100RS or the 750 K75S/SS models! The only advantage it would appear to offer over the original is weight – but on power, comfort or value it comes a poor second.

Further down the scale the R80 and R80RT models are respectable performers and, by BMW standards, offer good value for money. But round Donington neither did much to excite me.

Now for the R65. With the formula of R80 running gear and an engine less powerful than the earlier twin shock R65, the new 650 is without doubt the wooden spoon of the current BMW range. Just like the old R45 before it, the new R65 is gutless in the extreme and I for one was glad when my riding time on this model was up – enough said?

This leaves the R80G/S trial bike. One of my all-time favourite test bikes, around Donington its high braced bars and knobbly tyres placed one at a distinct disadvantage – something I had never noticed out on the road. Even so, its gutsy engine and controllability made it run a very close second to the standard R80 as my best boxer of the Donington test day.

But without a doubt my top rating goes to the K75S/SS which at Donington was a runaway winner, followed by the K75C. So, under the admittedly controlled environment of a traffic-free race circuit, the K-Series would appear to offer a most definite improvement in virtually every respect over the classic flat twin concept!

I am quite expecting enraged letters from boxer buffs – but when did *you* last try all the current BMW range, back-to-back?

Left: **Best of the bunch, the K75S Special.**

Other People's Test Quotes

K75C *Motorcycling Weekly* 29 October 1985.
'The engine is so smooth, responsive and refined it is in danger of becoming a modern classic. And it even looks better than the K100 lump with much better proportions'.

K75S *Motor Cycle News* 9 July 1986.
'Before trying the S, I would not have believed a BMW could have been such fun to ride hard and fast. The S puts a new dimension on BMW's range and I hope it is a taste of things to come'.

K100RS *Bike* June 1984.
'In many ways the K100RS is a considerable improvement on the old R100RS. Its engine is smoother, stronger and liable to stay in tune much longer while being just as easy to service. Far better than this in many ways is the matching improvement in stability at all speeds and under a very wide range of differing loads. Its improved handling means that you are liable to see the previously unimaginable outside road test circles: people going crazy on a BMW'.

K75S American *Motor Cyclist* November 1986.

'You wouldn't expect a 25 percent reduction in displacement to make a motorcycle more fun to ride, but that's what has happened with the K-Series BMW's.

K100RT *Mayfair* January 1985.

'The RT is probably the best all-rounder given the needs of a British motorcyclist. If you're thinking of a possible return to motorcycling, you could do much worse. And not a lot better'.

K100RT Australian *Revs* January 1987.

'In comparison to the GTR (Kawasaki) the BMW is more comfortable, more stable at speed, has better suspension, is lighter, more frugal, faster and has more mid-range power. I know the K100RT isn't new, but it's still the best sports tourer around'.

K75C American *Cycle Guide* September 1986.

'BMW's K75C is a breath of fresh air on the American motorcycle scene, a welcome alternative in a market stuffed with narrow-focus quickly obsolete fad bikes. There are faster, better handling bikes around, but the K75C will probably be around a lot longer than any of them and still be as satisfying years later as it is today. To me, the real appeal of the K75C is that it's a rational bike for motorcyclists who like to ride, not just be seen riding'.

10

Problems, Remedies, Modifications and Improvements

BMW is widely supposed to have spent between £35,000,000 and £60,000,000 on research and development for the K-Series bikes and, naturally, they are not denying it but, in spite of this investment and the millions of miles covered by hard riding testers as they abused the prototypes up the Alps and down the Autobahns, the fours and threes still had their problems.

It seems to be an immutable law of the motorcycling jungle that the customers will always find all sorts of faults that the factory testers never found. In fact, letting the customers carry out the R&D has been the standard practice for some manufacturers and even those who had done their best to sort out the most savage bugs before they let their latest model loose amongst the public have often overlooked some pretty fundamental mechanical disorders until they were pointed out by irritated purchasers.

The first LE Velocette was a classic case of just that sort of thing. Velocette's Directors firmly believed that 'racing improved the breed' and, accordingly, their ''everyman's motorcycle'' had a flat-twin engine that was almost, but not quite, indestructible with roller-type big-ends and four hefty ball races holding up the crankshaft. In the pink it churned out something like five feeble brake horse power and factory testers wrung the test bike's neck for several thousand miles with no hint of trouble, but when District Nurses bought them to go gently on their rounds and Distressed Gentlefolk treated them as pets as they pottered to the off-licence, the water-cooled engines never warmed up properly. Condensation soon set in, the oil turned to emulsion and the bearings quickly rotted, although barbarians could have thrashed the poor things round the TT Course for weeks and weeks and had no problems at all. Admittedly, Velocette were not quite in the same league as BMW when it came to spending money on research, but they were fine engineers who had built a lot of lovely motorcycles and it goes to show.

The K100s were so soon in trouble that one might be tempted to conclude that BMW knew quite well that they were far from perfect, but for sound commercial reasons kept strictly to their launching schedule in the certain knowledge that complaints would follow. By November 1983, only a *month* after the introduction of the basic K100, bikes were being recalled for attention to the rear brake master cylinders as owners were reporting that their brakes were locking on.

All BMW motorcycles, including the K-Series, are produced at the company's facilities in Spandau, West Berlin in what is claimed to be Europe's most modern motorcycle plant.

Even though a vast amount of money was spent on research and development followed by intensive testing, the early K-Series machines were not without their problems.

This was caused by the pistons sticking in the cylinders and the cure for this potential hazard was to fit new rear master cylinders with a Teflon coated piston and an external spring.

The rear brake disc was also modified at a very early stage, as the slotted discs got hot and cracked between the slots. All K-Series bikes are now fitted with a solid disc on the back wheel, except those with the drum, of course.

January '84 saw a starter freewheel redesign to prevent the starter slipping on engagement and around this time a batch of K100s were the subject of another Safety Related Recall to check for sub-standard plating on the helical gears driving the secondary engine shaft. This had, apparently, caused several engine seizures, but affected few machines sold here in Britain.

K100's being assembled on the Spandau production line.

The next recall came in the June of 1984 with a minor spate of jamming throttles, although this was not as dangerous as it might have been as it only happened when the bikes were started up. The trouble was traced to insufficient earthing of the starter button, the current preferring to use the throttle cable as an earth return instead of the official route. Surprisingly, this caused the outer cable to heat up and melt which caused the sticking throttle and the cure was an extra earth wire from the handlebars to the main earthing point beneath the tank.

From the very first, panic stricken owners soon complained of white smoke issuing from their new machine's capacious silencer and persisting for up to half a mile or so when the bike was started up. This is an unintentional design feature rather than a symptom of mechanical derangement and is caused by oil seeping past the piston rings. The same thing happens with the triples and it is worse when the bike has been left standing overnight, especially on the prop-stand as that allows the oil to run downhill instead of merely seeping. The strange thing is that the engines use very little oil, although they would appear to burn it in large quantities.

Concomitant to this and all the real disorders mentioned were several minor irritations. The brake-light micro switches regularly failed and were replaced under the warranties – until the warranties ran out – with switches which turned out to be identical. Not surprisingly these also failed. This went on for several months until supplies dried up and British switches are now standard. It is pleasant to record that the problem has gone away.

Fuel warning lights were a constant source of trouble from the start. An orange light came on when there were 7 litres of fuel left in the petrol tank and a red light came on when the reserve was down to 4 litres. That was the theory, anyway. In practice, the lights which worked, erratically, on the difference between the temperature of the petrol and the air inside the tank, shone their warnings for no apparent reason, sometimes when the tank was almost full. To effect a remedy BMW went over to a 'low-tech' float conversion, did away with the 7 litre warning light while still using the same speedo body less the orange bulb and with a 5 litre warning operating from the right hand window.

Alberto Criscuolo of BMW(GB) Ltd (right) discusses the technical details of a three-cylinder K75 engine with Mick Walker.

A mere month after the introduction of the basic K100, bikes were being recalled for attention to the rear brake master cylinders.

Early four-cylinder models had problems with the perforated rear disc. To cure this, all models with a rear disc now feature a type without holes on the braking area. One of the early cracked discs is illustrated.

The speedo was the cause of other aggravations. The instruments fitted to the early models sometimes gave slow readings and sometimes did not work at all. Or they could alternate between the two malfunctions due to a fault in the Printed Circuit Board, or PCB in high-tech jargon, which was soon modified.

Throttles stuck on some K100s due to current passing up the throttle cable rather than the starter button wiring. This was caused by insufficient earthing of the latter.

Original K-Series metal seat base was prone to rotting due to seat covering splitting and letting water in.

Some days it did not seem to matter much if the speedo worked or not as one could not read it due to condensation which misted up the glass. At least the British dealers put it down to condensation, drilling holes in the body which let the damp air out and used anti-misting visor gel on the inside of glass, but Spandau had a different theory. They were convinced that rain was getting in through the trip adjuster and they modified the instrument housing to keep the water out, although the dealers said it was not getting in and their simple methods had already cured the trouble.

A fourth recall took place in August 1985, involving all the K100 and K100RS models sold to date, which kept the dealers very busy. The problem on this occasion was defective ignition control units which had been misbehaving on a massive scale and causing more potential danger by cutting off the sparks completely or just failing to supply two cylinders; a situation not unlike an aircraft engine failure during take-off if the rider should be overtaking on a narrow road in the face of briskly moving traffic. There were even cases of brand new bikes that would not start for demonstration rides during showroom introduction parties. It turned out that the units had been too well sealed which caused internal condensation.

The ignition unit recall coincided with an in-house campaign to change the fuel pumps for a more powerful version. The pumps had not given any trouble in cool climates, but were replaced as it was found that hot sunshine could overheat the petrol in the tanks and bring on fuel injection problems. The new, uprated, pumps were fitted as a precaution in the interest of uniformity and they cured the carburation problem although they did not cool the fuel. To this end the gaiters sealing the fork leg apertures in the fairings of the K100RTs were removed and wind deflectors fitted in their place in order to direct a stream of cooling air around the petrol tank. In heavy traffic some after-market fairings can overheat the fuel.

In-line fuel filters breaking up inside the tank were a problem for quite some time. The fuel system is pressurized with a full flow return for unused fuel and any leakage in the system reduces pressure, causing poor performance and bad starting. The pressed alloy bodies of the original filters were extremely thin and split at the end seams. And they were even thinner where they had been date-stamped by the manufacturer, which proved to be another source of leaks. The problem still occurs, occasionally, but is easily corrected by fitting a much stronger filter.

The original fuel filler caps had a nasty habit of collecting rain water around the locking button and when the cap was opened the water fell into the tank. Apparently this did not matter all that much as the filter in the fuel pump would not let the pump pass water, if you will excuse the term, but owners were unhappy with diluted fuel. It was also possible to break the locking button by pressing it too hard – not difficult to do with freezing hands – and a modified design of fuel cap was eventually supplied on a generous basis, even outside warranty.

In terms of complication and expense, to customers and BMW itself, the most serious problem of all arose when the divided driven gear on the secondary engine shaft started to give trouble. This was

In terms of complication and expense to customers and BMW themselves, the most serious problem arose when the divided shaft started to give trouble. This . . .

. . . was due to the loss of tension in the circlip-type spring. Oddly, this was caused by the installation of too strong a spring.

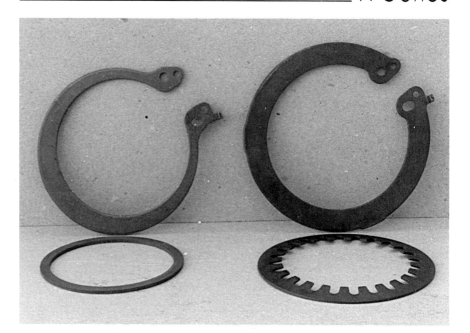

due to loss of tension in the circlip-type spring between these gears, allowing the narrow gear to flutter and make a noise much like a 'shot' big-end. This uncontrolled and independent movement wore the spring and let the two gears rub together under pre-load, causing them to bind. Oddly, the problem was caused by the installation of too strong a spring. This was rectified, quite simply, by the fitting of a softer spring and a new bearing on the output shaft to reduce the pre-load on the gears. The only major drawback was that this required a total engine strip-down.

Mileage was not a major factor in the life span of the crucial spring. And the onset of its collapse was unpredictable, depending as it did on how the bike was ridden. Naturally, the fault was put right free of charge on bikes still under warranty and even outside warranty for one-owner fours with a full service history and not too many miles behind them. In Britain BMW agreed to contribute 70% of the cost of the replacement parts for high mileage, second owner bikes, but the job could still cost something in the region of £400.

Many owners of the early K100 Series bikes complained of knocking noises from the forks, a phenomenon that dated back to the 'boxer' twins of 1981. The damper valve block was held into the bottom of each fork stanchion by a circlip which allowed the block to move, very slightly, up and down. Fitting slender shims failed to stop the movement for any length of time as the shims soon fell to bits. In September 1985 the factory introduced a new design of damper valve block with a shim 2mm thick which stopped the movement and the knocking, but this was classified as an improvement, instead of being a 'mod'.

In August 1986 there was another recall, this time because there had been several cases of throttles jamming open at 3,500 – 4,000rpm, which made a deep impression on the riders so affected and caused at least one accident in Britain. BMW assumed that the throttle cables had kinked due to an awkward angle at the throttle bank and ordered that they should be checked for kinking, but British dealers found that the midway cable adjusters had a tendency to slacken off, allowing the inner cable to drop out through the outer cable stop, and they changed the cables, making very sure that the locknuts were very firmly tightened.

Exhaust heat shields breaking off the K100S due to the onslaught of corrosion and vibration upon the mounting brackets is an unsolved problem, although the transmission of vibration to the riders of the fours – the threes are very smooth – has been considerably reduced by modification to the footrest plates. Originally, they were rubber mounted but they are now rigidly attached to the gearbox shell and 'Dr Martin's' type air-cushioned, anti-vibration footrest-rubbers insulate the rider's feet. In fact, the vibration of the fours can be markedly diminished in some cases, now that dealers are authorised to balance the secondary engine shaft on a balancing machine.

Corrosion has never been a major problem on any two-wheeled BMW, but the top frame rails of the K100RT/LT models are rather prone to surface rust due to damp being trapped beneath the seat. And the early K100s suffered from corrosion of the metal seat pan; the softness of the deep seat-padding caused the seat covering to split allowing water to get in. Late in 1984 a new seat was introduced with thinner, harder, padding which cured the splitting and fractionally reduced the effective seat height which had been the object of some criticism from owners who had found it hard to touch the ground. When the K75 came out it had a seat which looked very much the same, but which had a better grab handle and a plastic base. All the K-Series BMWs, both threes and fours, with the exception of the deluxe K100LT, now have this type of seat.

The cam covers have sometimes been a minor nuisance as they employ two re-useable rubber seals which tend to leak, but BMW do have a cure for this; a silicon based sealant at £27 a tube! However, to be fair, this problem has now been largely overcome by improving quality control at Spandau.

Other than the alterations mentioned which were initiated as remedies for specific problems, the majority of which were minor, maddening to live with and inevitable in any new machine, there have been remarkably few departures from the original designs. In 1985 harder valve seats were specified to cope with increased combustion chamber temperatures, a consequence of legislation against the use of leaded fuel. And since May 1987 all clutch splines have been nickel plated as a precaution against seizure. The only major changes have been the development of the Sporttuned suspension, which we discussed in Chapter 6, the use of radial tyres and the development of the ABS anti-lock braking system as an optional refinement.

Radial tyres are, at present, only offered on the special Motorsport edition of the K100RS and are reported to effect a marked improvement in the road holding. That being the case, we can assume that radials would improve the road holding of the entire

K-Series range at the upper levels of performance and may well be offered as an option in the not too distant future.

Radial tyres, roughly speaking, cost 50% more than conventional motorcycle tyres but, road holding apart, they have their compensations. Without delving too deeply into tyre technology, their main advantages are high speed stability and increased mileage. Even the best of cross ply tyres will 'grow' significantly at speed by as much as $3/8$in (9.5mm), distorting to a 'pointed' profile, lessening the contact patch, or 'footprint', and dramatically increasing wear. Radials distort much less – 300% less according to Pirelli – do not overheat and justify their higher price by lasting half as long again. They also have a large, more defined footprint, giving greatly improved grip under all circumstances, particularly in the rain.

The development of radial tyres for two-wheeled vehicles has great potential for improving rider safety, although it could be argued that all they really do is to present more opportunities to fall off at higher speed. This criticism may be levelled at systems to prevent the wheels from locking under heavy braking, but BMW's own ABS, unveiled at the Cologne Show in September 1986, is undoubtedly the most significant advance in safety that the motorcycle world has

Radial tyres improve the handling. Michelin even organised an event called *The Radial Day* on 8th May 1987 at Donington Park race circuit to prove the point.

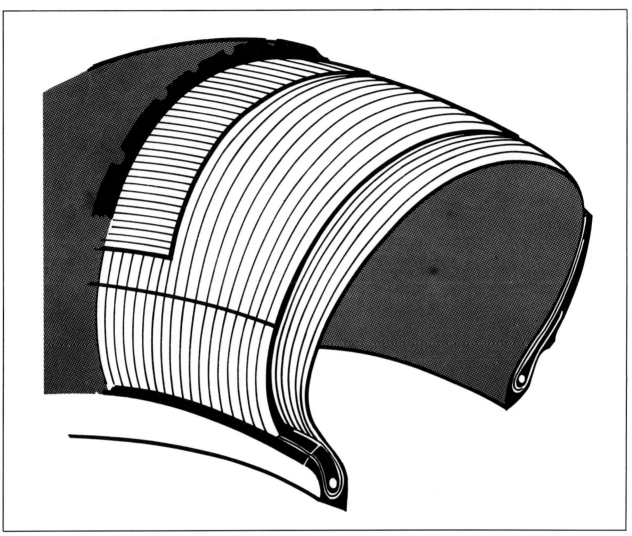

Construction of a radial motorcycle tyre. Its requirements differ considerably from the four-wheeled variety.

seen for many years. After all, the majority of serious motorcycle accidents occur at crossroads and at road junctions where the ability to slam the brakes on and not become another road accident statistic must improve our chances of survival on car – and truck – infested roads.

BMW itself has put it very well . . . "What really counts with ABS is the greater safety in emergencies, which is particularly important for the motorcycle rider. The first and foremost task of ABS is therefore to ensure absolute safety without the wheels locking, irrespective of road conditions. And precisely this objective has been reached far beyond the requirements of the average rider. While a top-notch rider might just be able to apply the brakes with the same efficiency on dry asphalt, ABS can cope with road surfaces varying rapidly and very substantially in their frictional coefficient, controlling the brakes at a speed far superior to human reflexes. Even if

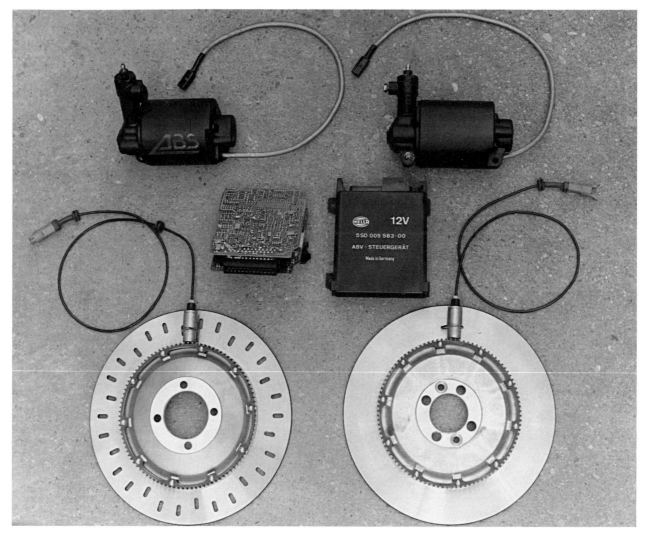

ABS anti-lock braking system. Developed by the Bavarian company FAG Kugelfischer on behalf of and in cooperation with BMW.

puddles, gravel, sand or oil suddenly appear on a hard and dry surface, ABS will respond quickly enough to prevent the wheels from locking. As long as he is riding in a straight line, the rider can therefore apply ABS brakes in full without the slightest fear of a wheel locking, thus achieving minimum stopping distances even if he is not very experienced. Particularly on slippery roads, the rider can achieve a retardation that even experienced test riders previously regarded as "almost impossible". It even works well on water-flooded black ice – "The kind of road that you can hardly walk on, let alone ride a motorcycle."

BMW's experiments with anti-lock braking systems began in 1978 when an R100RS was fitted with an adaptation of the ABS developed for their cars, but this required extensive modifications to the motorcycle's brakes and was very cumbersome. Feed-back at the brake levers varied from irritating to almost unendurable and BMW abandoned the car system as being too crude, although they did not put it quite like that but stated that it had not proved "compatible with the sensitive behaviour of a motorcycle."

They also experimented with a hydro/mechanical system developed in Britain, but it was not satisfactory as the actuating mechanisms increased the unsprung weight to an unacceptable degree and it could not control brake input below 6mph (10km/h). In the end they chose the electronic/hydraulic anti-lock device developed by FAG Kugelfischer of Bavaria as it was easy to connect to motorcycle brakes without any of the drawbacks mentioned.

This system is based on impulse sensor gears, each with 100 teeth, carried on the inside of the front and rear brake discs, passing information on wheel speed at a rate of 200 messages for each revolution of the wheel to a central electronic control unit. This enables the control unit to determine the degree of wheel deceleration within a certain period and activate a pressure modulator continuously reducing hydraulic pressure in the brake cylinders until the risk of wheel locking has passed. This happens 7 times a second while the rider keeps the brakes on hard until the speed drops below 2.5mph (km/h), with no feed-back to the levers as a valve prevents the reflow of brake fluid. In controlling the rear brake, the system takes into account the speed of the front wheel and this ensures that slowing caused by the closing of the throttle or a downward change of gear is not interpreted as braking action.

The two electric-motor pressure modulators are fairly heavy items at 8.4lbs (3.8kg) each and for this reason they are situated near the footrests, at the C of G, where they will have the least effect upon the handling.

The electronic control unit, made by Hella, is housed within the bike's tail section. It has two separate control lines for both wheels, operating intermittently at 10 second intervals. While one line is working the other supervises by passing information to a central processor unit. The voltage of the electronic system, the sensors and the pressure modulators are also supervised. In the event of a defect, two red lights will start flashing in the cockpit to tell the rider that, while his brakes still work, he will have to act as the anti-lock device until the fault is rectified. He can switch the flashing lights to a permanent red light which will not be too distracting.

The team developing the ABS gave considerable thought to maintenance and servicing. Using a test light, a BMW dealer or specialist can detect any deficiency present in the system and whether it involves one of the two sensors, the pressure modulators or the control box. All he has to do is to replace the faulty unit.

Originally scheduled to be introduced in 1987, but held up for a year due to problems with the failure warning lights – apparently the lights were coming on although the system had not failed – the ABS is now available, though only as an option on the K100 series at the present time. BMW say that it will not be possible to 'retrofit' due to the high cost factor. In the United Kingdom ABS will add £595, including VAT, to the price of a new bike. Very modest, considering the enormous sums that BMW have spent on R&D and less than the retail price in Germany. Neither BMW(GB) or its dealers will be

Compared with a standard machine, the rider of a motorcycle equipped wth ABS can ride without the worry of wheel locking under heavy braking as this photograph shows – the machine on the right does not have ABS!

Above right: View showing nearside of machine equipped with ABS. Evident from this shot is the 100-tooth impulse generator gear on the rear wheel – there is also a similar one on the front.

Right: Right hand ABS and rear brake master cylinder.

making money from the system as Pat Myers regards it as a safety feature from which it would be indefensible to make a profit. According to all published tests, it works astonishingly well and has to be worthwhile.

Visual changes have been few, at least until the introduction of the K75S Special and the K75. The Compact Drive System of the original K100 was left in natural alloy, but with a black sump and silencer heat shield. The K100RS and K100RT models followed suit, while the alloy fork legs were unprotected until mid '84 when they were painted black. The engine and transmission units of the K75-Series were also left in natural alloy until the K75 and the K75S Special made their debut at the Cologne Show in September 1986 with them painted black. A brilliant piece of marketing to make a feature, and a profit, out of something which, from a practical point of view, should have been part and parcel of the standard bikes. Although there is no denying that the natural alloy is attractive and makes the bikes look lighter and less massive.

The K75S Special also has black rims. The Motorsport editions of the K100RS have black engines and black rims, while the K100LT has a black engine, but with natural alloy rims.

The information in this chapter has been checked out by four separate dealers. One wrote . . . "I am not sure if I am supposed to condone this catalogue of faults of the early 'Ks'. It's accurate enough, but I think more emphasis should perhaps be placed on the

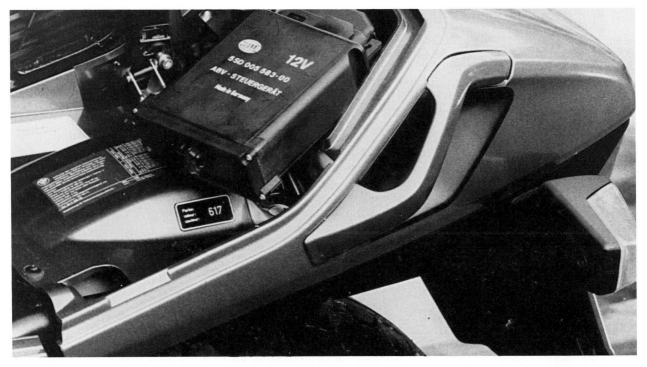

ABS electronic box produced by Hella is housed under the dual seat.

virtually trouble-free models built from '86 onwards. Some we see with very high mileages and still giving good service.''

Certainly the K100s are now extraordinarily reliable in every way, in addition to their other virtues. And from the very first the K75-Series triples have given very little trouble, but this book is meant to be a dispassionate assessment and not a mindless hymn of praise.

11

Servicing and Maintenance

Over the last few years BMW(GB) has been busily creating a car-type franchise of carefully selected dealers who, in many cases, specialize in motorcycles manufactured by BMW to the exclusion of all other makes. This similarity to the upper reaches of the motor trade with its glossy showrooms extends to servicing and maintenance, ensuring survival for the dealers and good service for the customers.

In contrast, the Japanese have encouraged discounting on a massive scale, often by firms who have no servicing or parts facilities and no intention of installing any! This short-sighted policy has caused carnage amongst dealers large and small alike and, sadly, it has been the dealers who felt they had a duty to provide a proper back-up service who have suffered most.

On the other hand, BMW actively discourage DIY enthusiasts from working on their own K-Series bikes, with the exception of a few simple tasks described in detail in the handbooks. One may cynically regard this attitude as part and parcel of their well-developed profit motive, but as both a onetime dealer and importer and the owner of a K75S, I (Mick Walker) can appreciate both points of view.

Editors of motorcycle magazines get lots of letters asking why no factory workshop manuals for the K-Series are currently available. After all, factory manuals are available for most Japanese machines, although how much actual use they are is open to debate due to the complexity of many of the engines and the cost of special tools. Quite apart from the difficulty of obtaining spares and the high prices charged for them.

There is, in fact, an official manual for the K-Series; all 600 pages of it, produced by BMW itself on micro-film. They forbid their agents to sell it to the public, but some of them will help you out and sell you the two sheets of film, each with 300 pages encompassed in a space roughly 5 inches by 4 inches, for anything from £6 to £15, plus VAT. The films are little use without a scanner as they must be magnified some fifty times to make them readable. And the information they contain is largely academic unless you are a skilled mechanic with a lot of special tools.

Whilst it is possible to rebuild a 'boxer' engine by improvising the odd tool, the K-Series engines are a different matter altogether and in 70% of operations special tools are needed. The tools required to complete a total engine rebuild for a three or four cost something in the region of £250. Similarly, £200-worth of special tools are needed to rebuild a gearbox, £300-worth for overhauling a rear axle and a further £30-worth for the forks. There is little doubt that a skilled engineer with a well-equipped workshop could make up the tools, but he would still need a gauge for balancing the throttle bank and they cost from £50 to £100. A meter is essential for adjusting the ratio of fuel to air and prices range from £250 to £1000, while the equipment necessary for the proper tuning of the fuel injection system costs £700 to £800.

The desire to mess about with motorcycles is not world-wide but seems to be a peculiarly British trait, probably because British motorcycles have traditionally needed lots of loving care to keep them on the road however good – or bad – they may have been in

K100 Series 987cc (70x67mm) engine.

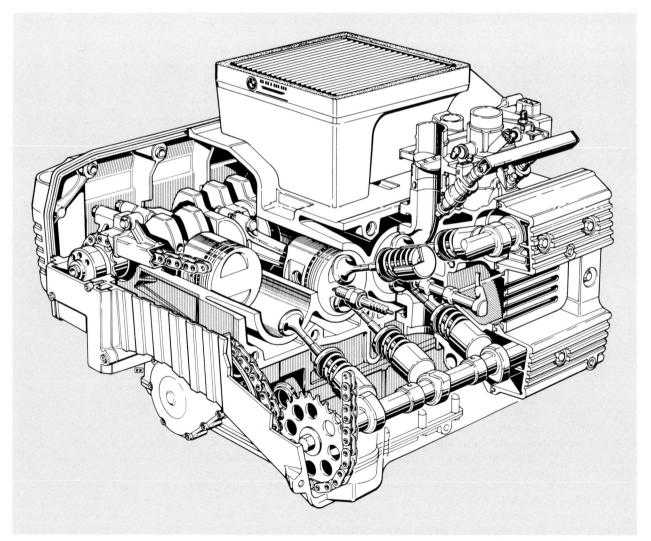

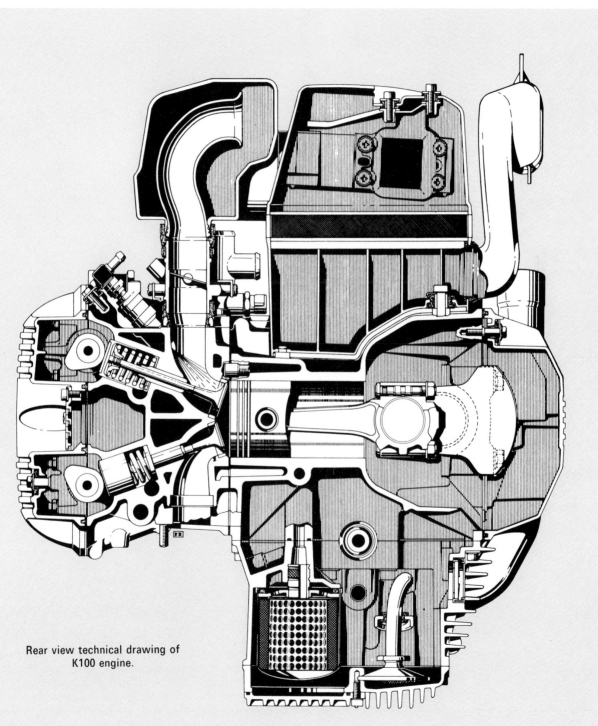

Rear view technical drawing of
K100 engine.

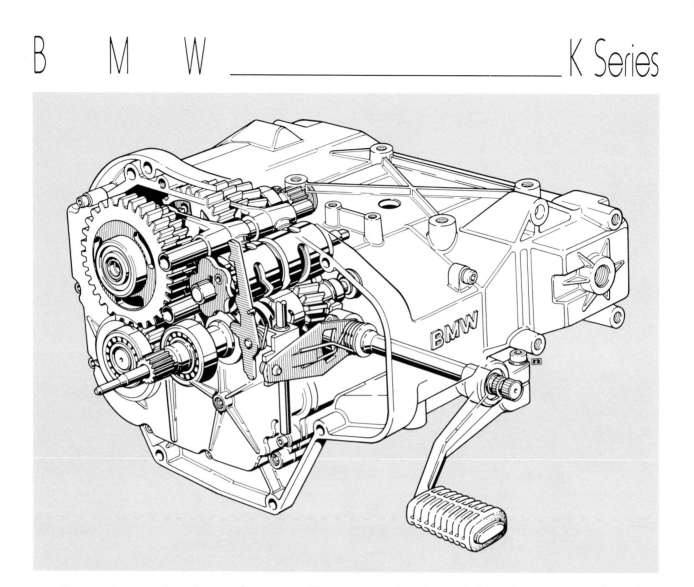

Five-speed gearbox shared by both the three and four-cylinder models.

other ways. The average Continental rider does not care for grimy fingernails. Nor do the people that BMW are attracting into motorcycling with two page advertisements in up-market general interest magazines and this fits in well with BMW's own plans for servicing its motorcycles. Few of us are skilled mechanics and they do not want a lot of bodgers fiddling about and spoiling the performance of their well set-up machines. One incompetent is bound to do a lot of damage and then blame BMW and that sort of thing could harm their reputation.

In spite of their reluctance to have the customers laying untutored hands on their machines, every new BMW comes with a superb toolkit which is more than adequate to carry out the tasks sanctioned by the handbooks. The handbooks, incidentally, are beautifully produced and contain a lot of useful information under five main headings: *Operating Instructions; Safety Hints; Riding Hints and Minor Repairs; Specifications and Technical Descriptions* and *Care and Maintenance,* followed by a section made up of *Service Confirmations.*

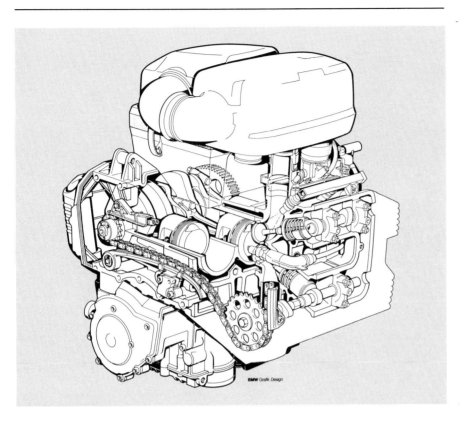

Shorter K75 Series 740cc unit.

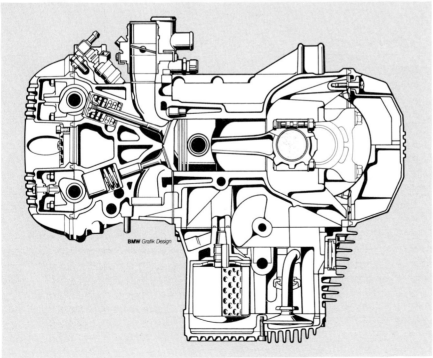

Rearward view of K75 engine
assembly.

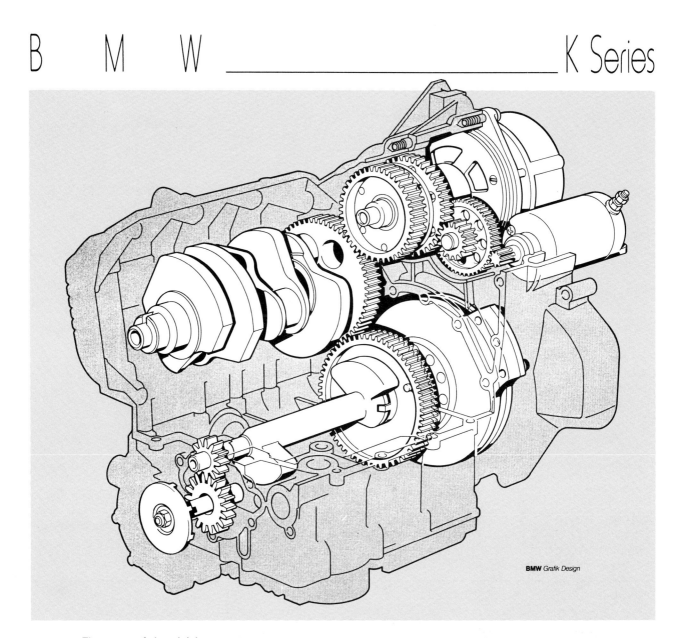

BMW *Grafik Design*

The secret of the triple's distinctively smooth running is thanks largely to the balancer shaft. The rearmost crank web doubles as a gearwheel to drive the shaft at engine speed.

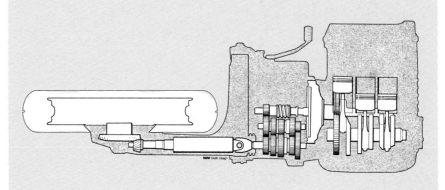

K75 Compact Drive System.

Handbooks . . .

They also contain a modicum of nonsense under the sub-heading *Beauty Care.* "Most motorcycle owners are familiar with the way an admiring crowd – of all ages – gathers around a sparkling, clean motorcycle whenever it is parked for a few minutes. Who would not be just a little proud to receive this public recognition of his efforts?' Who indeed? But maybe things are different in West Germany.

There are precise instructions for removing and replacing wheels and repairing punctures in the tubeless tyres with the kit provided; for changing bulbs and fuses; checking spark plugs; topping up with coolant and for adjustment of free travel at the clutch lever.

These step-by-step procedures for the jobs that owners may well have to do are followed by equally precise instructions for jobs that owners have official blessing to perform, if they feel they really must. These are confined to changing oils throughout the CDS and the front forks, renewing the air cleaner, adjusting brakes and checking the battery. The warning that . . . 'Your motorcycle is equipped with a microprocessor-controlled high performance digital

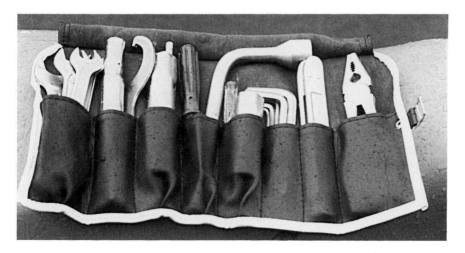

. . . and toolkits are without equal in the motorcycle world.

ignition system. As a result, it can be highly dangerous or even fatal to touch any live component when the engine is running' . . . might have been displayed more prominently. For instance on the cover instead of on page 30 where it might be much too late to save an owner from a nasty shock. But on the whole both the K-Series handbooks are sensible, well printed documents on 112 pages of heavy, glossy paper.

Fuel injection system requires correct setting up procedures and test equipment.

The cost of service and repairs to a K-Series bike – and to the 'boxers' – is calculated on a system of Flat Rate Units, 12 units to the hour, and charges in Britain vary from £1.35 to £1.60 per unit, adding up to labour charges of £16.20 to £19.20 per hour, plus VAT. Renewing a head gasket on a K100, for example, is rated at 46 Flat Rate Units which, charged at £1.50 per unit or £18 per hour, is £69, plus materials and VAT. The same job on a K100RS and a K100RT is rated at 58 and 60 FRUs respectively due to the added complication of the fairings.

To give you an idea of the cost of labour on some other jobs,

adjusting the steering of a K100RS is rated at 5 units. Renewing the clutch is rated at 31 units; renewing the clutch cable rates 8 units; changing the brake fluid 4 units; timing the ignition 14 units; adjusting the valve clearances 9 units and renewing the starter motor 7 units. The times involved are reasonable – BMW mechanics may think them pretty tight. But in terms of hard cash at the rates quoted, plus materials and VAT, they should be of interest to anybody contemplating buying a secondhand K-Series bike and hoping to run it inexpensively.

Servicing is scheduled at 6 monthly intervals, or 5,000 miles (7,500km). The major services, which are termed Inspections, being due at yearly intervals or 10,000, 20,000, 30,000 miles and so on. 17 units are allocated for a 5,000 mile service for a K100, 19 for a K100RS and 26 for a K100RT, while the K75C and K75S are rated at the same amount of units as a K100.

The total cost of a 5,000 mile service to a K100RS, charged at £1.50 per unit, works out approximately as follows . . .

Above left: **Lifting the tank gives access to radiator filler cap, ignition control unit and various relays and sensors.**

Above: **Visible in this shot are the injectors, bar and throttle bank (left), whilst centred right are the ignition coils.**

Labour	28.50
Oil change kit	9.80
Engine oil	9.00
4 Spark plugs	6.60
Valve clearance shims (say 2) at 1.60	3.20
Sundries (Grease, sprays, etc)	300
	60.10
Value Added Tax (VAT)	9.01
TOTAL	£69.11

A 10,000 mile Inspection for a K100RS is allocated 41 Flat Rate Units – the K100 and the K100RT are each allocated 37 and 49. An Inspection involves the use of a Service Kit, costing £34 plus VAT.

Engine oil change kit	*1*
Spark plugs	*4*
Air filter	*1*
Fuel filter	*1*
Engine oil filler plug 'O' ring	*1*
Gear box oil level plug washer	*1*
Gear box drain plug washer	*1*
Rear axle drain plug washer	*1*
Rear axle oil level plug washer	*1*

This means that an Inspection for a K100RS, charged at £1.50 per unit, will cost approximately:

Labour	*61.50*
Service Kit	*34.00*
Oil (eng, g/box, axle, fork)	*18.00*
Valve clearance shims (say 2 at 1.60)	*3.20*
Sundries (Grease, sprays, etc)	*3.00*
	119.70
Value Added Tax (VAT)	*17.95*
TOTAL	*£137.65*

At 10,000 miles it is very likely that the bike will need new disc pads. These cost £17 per disc, plus VAT. Labour charges, at £1.50 per unit, are £4.50 for changing all 4 front disc pads and £3.00 for changing the one set at the rear which is more difficult. Therefore the total charge including VAT is £67.27.

On a 5,000 mile service, calculated at £1.50 per Flat Rate Unit, the most that you can save by doing it yourself would be the labour charge, sundries and the VAT, which add up to £36.22. On a 10,000 mile Inspection you could save £74.17. In theory, the jobs take a trained mechanic, working in ideal conditions with all the proper tools, 1 hour 36 minutes and 3 hours 42 minutes respectively. We suspect that they would take the average owner a lot longer, but it all depends on how you like to spend your leisure time or how you cost your labour. However much you may enjoy working on your bike, it still leaves you with the problem of servicing the ignition system and the fuel injection. Certainly you pay your money, but you do not seem to have much choice.

12

Accessories

BMW offer an enormous variety of accessories for the K-Series machines. Elegant and large capacity integral cases, top cases, city cases, tank bags, luggage rolls, luggage racks, extra comfort seats, knee cushions, heated handlebar grips – highly recommended – radios, windscreens and a great deal more. All of this equipment is of the usual super quality and all of it expensive, as you might expect. Brochures and price lists covering the range are available from showrooms but, as a quick example of the costs, a tank bag is priced at £94.93, a top case at £117.16 and a windscreen for a K100 at £163.19, all including VAT.

K100 with factory optional extras: windshield, additional headlights, crash bars, tank bag, touring panniers and Nivomat rear suspension unit.

B M W

BMW Touring panniers – 2.45 cu
ft capacity.

Touring First Class – K100RT with
tank bag, luggage roll, touring
panniers – hang on female pillion
is *not* available!

For the most part, other makers of accessories have been content to leave that section of the 'after market' to BMW themselves, presumably because they cannot compete on quality at a satisfactory profit margin. But due to the high prices of original equipment, BMW are vulnerable when it comes to accident replacements or fairings for their unfaired bikes and in this sector of the market there is a lot of competition. This stems not only from German manufacturers, but from British, Irish, Italian and Spanish sources.

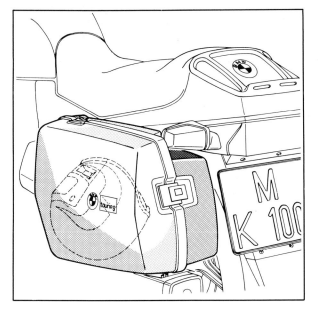

Right: **BMW City case – 1.4 cu ft capacity.**

Above: **Touring panniers will even hold a full-face helmet.**

In this chapter we will have a look at some of the alternatives to BMW's own fairings and at a representative selection of equipment also currently on offer. But before we do, it might be wise to remind prospective buyers of proprietary items that BMW at Spandau shaped their fairings in a wind tunnel with stability and safety very much in mind. The screen area of the standard fairing of a K100RS is designed to be a spoiler and exerts a downward pressure that counteracts a front end tendency to lift at speed and, if you intend to use the full performance of your three or four, you would be well advised to arrange a test ride on a similar machine fitted with the fairing you intend to buy.

Acrybre Products

Acrybre make a full touring fairing to fit the K75 and K100, the only difference being in the design of the plastic coated metal fitting brackets. It is supplied complete with a RT type mounting kit for the speedometer and rev counter as the instrument nacelle must be removed and the headlamp mounted on the fairing. The only other parts to be removed are the flashing indicators and the fairing can be fitted to a bike within an hour.

It has internal mouldings with storage pockets and leathercloth covers and screens of varying height are readily available. Acrybre offer free fitting at the works and this has the distinct advantage that the customer can test ride his machine with an adjustable windscreen in order to determine the ideal screen to suit his height and riding style. The firm will then produce a screen in clear or tinted Acrylic while he waits. The price is £350 plus VAT.

Acrybre now offer a full range of replacement screens for all K-Series models, in various heights.

Acrybre Products touring fairing for K100. The British company also manufactures clear or tinted replacement screens in a variety of heights.

Alco

Alco are a Dutch firm producing the Speed 7 range of fairings, handlebar fairings and windscreens, top boxes and other items for Honda, Kawasaki, Suzuki and Yamaha machines, but include two useful taller screens for the K100RS and K100RT BMWs. They also make a fuel injection cover for all the K75s and K100.

The Speed 7 K100RS screen is 14cm (approximately $5^1/_2$ inches) higher than the standard screen, while the replacement for the K100RT screen is 7cm (roughly $2^1/_4$ inches) higher. Both screens are made of Acrylic. The RS screen is 3.5mm thick, while the RT version is 5mm thick. Both are slightly tinted and are distortion-free. The fuel injection covers are injection moulded ABS, the same material used for BMW's own panniers.

These three Speed 7 products are imported into Britain by Bob Porecha (see addresses). The K100RS replacement screen costs £62.41 and the K100RT replacement costs £67.50. Both prices are inclusive of VAT and postage.

Fournales France

Suspension units. See M R Holland (Distributors) Ltd

Holland

M R Holland (Distributors) Ltd

In the words of the Carlsberg advertisement M R Holland are 'probably' the biggest bike suspension specialist in the United Kingdom. They market Spax and Fournales monoshock rear units for K75 and K100 series bikes and the progressive fork springs made by Progressive Suspension Inc, of California.

The British Spax units come with a free 'C' spanner for adjusting pre-load, but cost £147. The units manufactured by the French Fournales firm are of the pump-up, oleopneumatic type with hydraulic damping. They are set up to cope with solo/duo use, but the air pressure has to be adjusted to carry heavy touring loads. They cost a whopping £317 each, while an original equipment monoshock costs £100. A remarkable departure from the after market norm where alternative equipment is invariably cheaper than BMW's own products.

The progressive fork springs cost £46.50 for the pair. The makers claim that they eliminate front end sag, reduce nose diving under braking, allow the forks to utilize their full travel, increase the rider's comfort and improve stability. Prices include VAT and P&P.

Krauser

Krauser are a major force in German motorcycling. They are the world's largest manufacturer of pannier equipment and are very much involved in motorcycle racing. For K-Series BMWs only panniers, pannier frames, topcases, and fairings are imported here by Krauser Imports Ltd of Basingstoke (See addresses). They are available through a network of some 200 dealers throughout Britain, or direct from the importers.

The panniers are extremely practical and elegant. Injection moulded in two halves with an aluminium centre section, they are probably the ultimate in motorcycle luggage. The cost of Krauser K2 panniers in 30 or 42 litre capacities is a little over £200 a pair, depending on the source. Neat and simple pannier frames cost around £75, while 35 or 46 litre K2 Topcases cost around £122 and £131 respectively.

Krauser fairings designed to fill the gap between the sporting and the touring fairings made by BMW are available for the K75 and K100. Sections can be removed for summer riding. Of high quality, as are all Krauser products, at around £675 these fairings are a great deal less expensive than original equipment. All prices mentioned include VAT.

Motad

The silencer of the K100 has been almost universally condemned on aesthetic grounds, although it does its job extremely well. It imparts a quiet, if not particularly attractive, note to the exhaust and gives a good, smooth, power delivery. It is made of stainless steel and will probably outlast the bike, but it has a heat shield that tends to work loose and rattle and most people hate the sight of it.

Motad offer a much better looking silencer, which is round instead of square with rounded corners and which matches, or marginally improves upon the standard power curve. It has been tested in Europe by Government agencies and has been granted a type-approval certificate to prove that it conforms to the latest EEC legislation on noise pollution.

The company have developed a special process which enables them to chrome-plate stainless steel as it discolours with the heat and this process can also be applied to silver or black options to match the finish of a bike. There is no need for any heat shield; the unit is slightly shorter than the standard item so that the wheel can be removed without lifting the tail section of the mudguard and ground clearance is improved.

Prices are £99.00 in silver chrome, or £115.00 in black, both including VAT.

Pichler

Pichler – pronounced Pickler – are a large and successful German company who specialise in fairings for all the leading makes and more than 50,000 of their products have been sold through a worldwide network of 6,000 dealers. In addition to making half and full depth fairings for the 'boxers', they offer a very striking full fairing for the K75 and K100, designated the PK1. This has a single headlamp, two streamlined mirrors, integral flashing indicators and a

Pichler, one of Germany's most successful after-market motorcycle fairing manufacturers, provides comprehensive streamlining for both K75 (illustrated) and K100 models.

sophisticated ventilation system. They also make a fairing for the back of these machines, known as the Raceback PK1. This has a single seat which is 2 inches (5cm) lower than the standard item with a lock-up hump behind the seat providing useful extra storage space, while the side panels can be easily removed in order to fit pannier cases.

A 'spoiler fender' or 'front mudguard', which Pichler claim increases downward pressure on the front wheel, is also available. The British importers are Tony's Motorcycles of Prestatyn (see addresses) and prices are £535 for the PK1, £395 for the Raceback and £40 for the front mudguard, all including VAT.

B M W

Long an object of dislike by
owners of the K100 machines was
the original silencer. As this
photograph proves, the Motad
replacement is much more
attractive.

Belly pan available from Profile
Fairings of Belfast for all
K75/K100's.

Profile Fairings

Profile Fairings of Belfast make a neat lower fairing for the K100 and the K100RS. It encompasses the sump and 'complements the lines and style of both motorcycles', as the brochure puts it. The fairing is manufactured from high quality, hand-laid glass fibre. It is available acid etched and primed for the best possible paint adhesion, a process carried out by BMW on all glass fibre items. Fairings colour-matched with BMW paint kits can be supplied. BMW paint kits cost £25 for a quarter litre, except for Motorsport Pearl White which costs around £45 per quarter litre. Primed fairings cost £65, colour-matched fairings cost £79, or £90 in Motorsport Pearl White. Add £4.50 to cover P&P.

Progressive Suspension Inc

Progressive fork springs for K-Series bikes. See M R Holland (Distributors) Ltd.

Rickman Motorcycle Accessories

Rickman's are probably the world's largest manufacturers of 'after market' fairings, but they make only one type of fairing for the K100 and K75C. Known as the type 24, it is a handsome touring fairing with a single headlamp, good protection for the rider's feet and a high screen. Screens are available clear, blue, smoked, or extra long

Type 24 – a full touring fairing
from the well known New Milton,
Hampshire concern, Rickman
Brothers.

in clear material. The shells are made from top quality glass reinforced plastic and the mounting brackets are fabricated from high grade mild steel finished in a tough black plastic coating. The fairing has two lockable glove compartments and is colour matched to BMW's own colours or left black or white.

Distributed by Fowlers (see addresses), prices of painted fairings are £362.20, plus VAT, while unpainted fairings are £310.08, plus VAT.

Spax

Suspension units. See M R Holland (Distributors) Ltd.

Sprint Manufacturing

Sprint Manufacturing of Wiltshire making fairings for Triumphs, Nortons, Velocettes, Ducatis and Moto Guzzis and are Britain's most prolific maker of sports and touring fairings for all sorts of BMWs. They make the Avon Avonaire, a period touring fairing for the R50, R60, the R69 and R69S; a 'Crusader' handlebar fairing; a 'Crusader' three-piece fairing; a K100RS-style twin headlamp fairing for the R45, R65 and R80ST; a 'Crusader' engine fairing/leg shield set for the R65LS; and a K100RS-style fairing, or a 'Metro' frame-mounted fairing for the 6/7 Models and the new R80.

1984 – early K100RS style fairing by Sprint Manufacturing – BMW threatened legal action . . .

Above: **Early Sprint RS** – style 2-headlamp design fitted to K75C.

Above right: **Late Sprint RT**-style two-headlamp fairing.

Late Sprint RS fairing – compare differences with original.

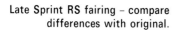

In addition to all these they make two single headlamp and two double headlamp sports or touring fairings for the K75 and the K100; a K100 combination-type seat complete with single seat, dual seat, tail/base unit and all fittings, and a lower, or engine, fairing to fit genuine BMW K100RS or RT fairings, the standard unfaired K100, their own RS-style fairing and the K75 range.

All Sprint products conform to a high standard. Screws, nuts and washers are made of stainless steel, brackets are black plastic coated and the fairings are constructed from glass fibre reinforced plastic. Single headlamp models utilise the original BMW light unit, while the twin headlamp versions are supplied with twin dipping 130mm Cibie halogen (120w high/110w low) units. Fairings are delivered in fully finished form, rather than as kits, with brackets loosely fitted in the right positions. Customers can have a special colour scheme, at extra cost, but fairings are normally supplied to order in BMW's own paint, with options of standard K75 or K100 indicators, or the K100RS mirrors with integral indicators.

The windscreen area of Sprint's RS style fairing differs markedly from BMW's design, and Sprint claim that their layout creates a lot less turbulence. But until mid 1986, when BMW objected, the lower half of the Sprint RS style fairing did bear a strong resemblance to the factory item. As litigation is a luxury that few people can afford, and they had been rather tactless and used the BMW logo, Sprint were forced to alter the design. They came up with a fairing in which the 'demarcation' line between the upper and the lower half runs upwards towards the rear of the machine, instead of downwards, matching the line of the K-Series tank, and resulting in an even better looking product.

The RT style touring fairing is made up of three main sections, and can be used without the lower foot protection section. They have built-in, double skinned, compartments with locking lids, and screens are available in height variations to suit all riders. The firm also make replacement screens for genuine BMW fairings, and for Sprint and Avon fairings.

Fairing prices are as follows, and include both VAT and the delivery charge. Single headlamp RS style £359. Double headlamp RS style £435. Single headlamp RT style £499. Double headlamp RT style £575. The combination seat costs £179, while the lower fairing is priced at £95.

TCP

TCP claims to be Spain's largest manufacturer of fairings and accessories. It supplies the fairings for the Spanish racing teams Kobas and Braun JJ Cobas, but only makes one fairing and an engine spoiler for K-Series bikes. In appearance the fairing is very similar indeed to BMW's own K100RS fairing. So similar, in fact, that one wonders why Sprint Manufacturing was singled out and forced to alter its design. Both the fairing and the spoiler are finished in BMW colours. No prices are available and they are not imported into Britain.

Wüdo K-Series fairing clearly based on BMW's own R100RS type. A similar fairing is offered in Britain by Ongar Motorcycles.

Wüdo

This German company are specialists in BMW accessories and publish a thick, A4-size catalogue listing a huge range of bolt-on 'goodies' and go-faster gear, although the bulk of it is meant for 'boxer' twins. For the K-Series bikes they offer, amongst other things, streamlined tail sections with double or single seats; engine spoilers for the K100RS; perspex 'ears' for widening the windscreen area; special rear suspension struts; rearset footrests with brakes and gear levers; an alternative instrument panel for the K100RS and the RT; oil pressure gauges; oil and water temperature gauges and special 2.50 or 2.75 x 3.50 section light alloy wheels. At present they offer fairings only for the 'boxer' twins.

Wüdo equipment is not imported into Britain.

Wulf Gerstenmaier

This West German company makes kits of specialised components for the K75 and the K100 intended to enhance their sporting image, in addition to providing some protection for the rider. The equipment for the K100 first appeared in 1985 and comprises a rakish, full-depth fairing in BMW's own red with a single headlamp, single mirror and a low windscreen. It was designed to collapse progressively on impact in a head-on crash. They also offer an abbreviated front mudguard, a new tail section with a single or a double seat and a complex, lightweight casting incorporating rearset footrests for the rider and the pillion passenger together with neat rearset brake and gear levers.

The K75 kit appeared in 1986. There is a handsome three quarter fairing with integral flashing indicators and a single headlamp. Finished in BMW's own silver paint, the fairing features an ingenious pivoting windscreen which allows the rider to adjust the airflow as required. The tail sections are available in matching colours, while the rearset assemblies are virtually the same. They also make an engine spoiler for the K100RS and K75S and the full fairing is available in silver with a striking pale blue/dark blue/red orange stripe. This striping can also be applied to the front mudguard, tank and tail section.

Wulf equipment is not imported into Britain.

Ultimate Source

To complete this section we feel we must include Ultimate Source, the Manchester mail order company who specialise in BMW accessories. Their glossy 64-page catalogue is a superb production and a must for all owners of R-Series and K-Series bikes. It covers an enormous range of top quality equipment and is available free of charge, on application. (See addresses.)

Wulf customising equipment not only includes fairing, but seat, side panels, front mudguard, handlebars and rear set foot controls.

Below left: For K100 owners who want a replica of their bike in the living room – kit makers Tamiya offer this 1/12th scale plastic kit which is very accurate.

Below: Ongar Motorcycles offered both this R100RT-type fairing (shown on a K75C) together with a R100RS version for the K-Series machines.

B M W

Addresses of Manufacturers, and of British Importers

Acrybre Products
10 Albany Road
Granby Ind Est
Weymouth
Dorset
Tel 0305 787498

Alco bv (frejo-groep)
Ph Foggstraat 24 - 7821
AK Emmen
Holland

The importers are:
Bob Porecha (BMW
Specialists)
303 Sydenham Road
London SE26 5EW
Tel 01 659 8860

Fournales France
20 route de Baziege
31320 Laberge
France
Tel (61) 75 74 52

The importers are:
M R Holland (Distributors)
Ltd
See Holland M R

**Holland M R
(Distributors) Ltd**
Unit 2 Benner Road
Wardentree Lane Ind Est
Spalding
Lincs
Tel 0775 66455

Krauser GmbH
Horsmannsberger Str 18
8905 Mering
West Germany
Tel 010 49 8233 1053

The importers are:
Krauser Imports Ltd
Unit 1, Grafton Way
West Ham Ind Est
Basingstoke
Hants
Tel 0256 57371

Motad International Ltd
Unit B
Invicta Trading Est
Hunts Lane
London E15 2QE
Tel 01 519 8686

Pichler
Kunststofftechnik GmbH
Postfach 13 56
Lauterbachstrasse 19
8330 Egtenfelden
West Germany

The Pichler importers are:
Tony's Motorcycles
8 Sandy Lane
Prestatyn
Clwyd
Tel: 07456 3455

Profile Fairings
15 Camberwell Terrace
Belfast BT15 3AS
Northern Ireland
Tel 0232 741020

**Progressive Suspension
Inc**
15661 "N" Producer Lane
Huntingdon Beach
CA 92649
USA
Tel (714) 898 2951

The importers are:
M R Holland (Distributors)
Ltd
See Holland M R

**Rickman Motorcycle
Accessories**
Stem Lane
New Milton
Hants BH25 5NW
Tel 0425 613838

*The Rickman distributors
are:*
Fowlers Motorcycles Ltd
2—12 Bath Road
Bristol
BS4 3DR
Tel 0272 770466

Spax Ltd
Telford Road
Bicester
Oxon OX6 0UU
Tel 08692 44771

The distributors are:
M R Holland (Distributors)
Ltd
See Holland M R

Sprint Manufacturing
30B Upton Lovell
Nr Warminster
Wiltshire
BA12 0JW
Tel 0985 50821

TCP
Carretera de Cornella, 144
08950 Esplagues de
Llobregat
Barcelona
Spain

Ultimate Source
Unit 3, Southern Street
Castlefield
Manchester M3 4NN
Tel 061 832 7196

Wüdo
Deutsche Str.98/100
4600 Dortmund – Eving 16
West Germany

Wulf Gerstenmaier
Im Steinernen Kreuz 14
7474 Bitz
West Germany

13

Sidecars

BMW has stated, very firmly, that sidecars must not be attached to any of the K-Series and there is a certain irony in this as BMWs, with their Rennsport 'boxer' engines, dominated European sidecar racing for very nearly twenty years. But in spite of this dire warning, heavy with the threat of instant negation of all rights under warranty, five firms offer sidecar conversions for K-Series bikes. The reason for BMW's disregard of glories past is, of course, the frame – or lack of it – but, properly converted, the Ks – and K100s in particular – are very suitable as sidecar tugs. Provided that you are keen on sidecar outfits, a form of transport that demands a high level of enthusiasm.

Sub frames, or entirely new frames, are the first essential for the fitting of a sidecar to a K100 or a triple. The CDS, which forms the mainstay of the standard set-up, is not stressed to cope with the kind of lateral forces generated by a 'chair'. Teledraulic forks are not ideal, partly for that reason and partly because the steering set-up of a sidecar outfit is quite different from a solo and the angle of the steering head has to be much steeper in order to reduce the trail. This explains why leading link front forks are *de rigueur* for all five manufacturers. Motorcycle tyres are not really suitable for sidecar outfits as the sidewalls were designed for a different and less stressful role. Car tyres are much better, but opinions differ as to the best wheel size. 15inch all round gives constructors a good choice of car tyres, but these radials do have their drawbacks as they tend to 'wander' slightly. On the other hand they make it easy to conform to European legislation which insists that vehicles must have the same tread pattern on each tyre.

EML

Complete machines from EML have held the sidecar moto-cross World Championship for several years and the Dutch company are now the largest manufacturer of sidecars. They produce 3,000 or so units in a year and sell large numbers to Japan, Australia and to the German police.

They make single-seater and side-by-side child/adult and double adult sidecars. Unlike the other manufacturers, they supply them in kit form, the kits comprising the sidecar body; the sidecar

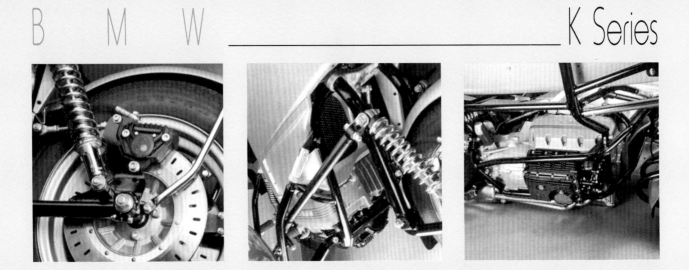

Above (left to right)
Earles-type front forks play an important role in the EML concept . . .
Sidecar fitting contributes to proving it is possible to add a third wheel.

K100RS modified for sidecar use by the Dutch EML company (main picture)

chassis with a brake and all the fittings; leading link front forks; three 15-inch wheels with fabricated spokes that are bolted to the rims complete with tyres and tubes and a disc brake for the 'chair' wheel. The kit for K-Series BMWs includes a complete new frame instead of just a sub-frame.

The British importers are E W Pinchbeck & Sons of Middle Wallop (see addresses) and they will sell the customer a kit for around £2,500, or fit the contents of a kit to the customer's machine. Fitting charges for K-Series BMWs are around £1000 to £1500.

The sidecar bodies are all black and painting or colour matching of the bike and sidecar costs around £200. All prices mentioned are subject to 15% VAT.

EML chair, using basic K100 as the basis.

Koch

Koch Motorrad GmbH produce a range of single-seater sidecars for both flat twin and K-Series BMWs. In addition the company buy and sell older BMWs. Rainer Koch is a great BMW enthusiast and was

Complete K100RT sidecar package
offered by Koch Motorrad GmbH
of West Germany.

personally in charge of the company's stand at the 1987 Milan Show. Besides sidecars, complete K100 and K100RT outfits with small wheels and special forks are offered as a package. Sales are made direct to customers; there are no distributors involved. Koch sidecars are not imported into Britain and no prices are available.

Unit Sidecars

Unit Sidecars of Sible Hedingham in Essex make two basic models, both to customers' requirements: a sporty single seater called the Hedingham and a side-by-side two seater, which looks very similar, called the Hedingham XL. The bodies are manufactured in heavy, 4oz fibreglass; the mudguards are a reinforced resin moulding, while the chassis are of welded steel construction with main members 2 inches (50mm) in diameter doubling as crash protection by encircling the body. Suspension is by torsion bar with an option of three thicknesses for a harder or a softer ride.

The Hedingham single seater with a tonneau, but no hood, a 16 inch wheel and a boot lid rack costs £1099. Extras include a hood which extends from the windscreen back across the boot, a quilted seat, a spot lamp and 2 inch diameter defender bar, a cast alloy wheel

15 or 16 inches in diameter and a tow hitch for a trailer. Together they add up to £407, but a Super Hedingham, which is a basic Hedingham with all the extras excepting the tow hitch, will cost you only £1375.

The Hedingham XL is priced at £1325. It comes with a fully-upholstered bench type seat, a 15 inch cast alloy wheel, a bigger boot and smaller hood. Hydraulic sidecar brakes for all three Hedinghams cost £250.

Unit makes a special sub-frame for K-Series BMWs which takes the sidecar fittings and the strain. It costs £197 and is also available with fittings for Watsonian or Squire sidecars. They also make leading link front forks to their own design. They cost £296.40 for a K100, plus a £65 fitting charge. All prices mentioned are subject to the inevitable 15% VAT.

Unit Sidecars produce various extremely attractive sporting chairs – plus a special sub-frame for K-Series machines and a leading-link front fork of their own design

VMC

VMC are a Dutch firm which specialises in ultra-lightweight chassis kits for sidecar motocross. The standard frame of their K100 outfit has been discarded in favour of a more elaborate and stronger structure. VMC's own leading link front forks and rear disc brake are fitted and their own 15-inch, 8-spoke cast wheels are substituted for the standard items. The sidecar is a reinforced fibreglass single-seater with trailing arm suspension, controlled by a Koni shock absorber and supported by another 15 inch VMC cast wheel.

All production has so far been of right hand outfits and VMC have been too busy supplying the Dutch and German police to build a left hand 'chair'. Consequently they are not imported into Britain.

Wasp Motorcycles

Rhind-Tutt's Wasp Company of Wiltshire is also deeply involved in sidecar moto-cross, but makes a touring child/adult sidecar and a

Leading link front forks. Made from Reynolds 531 tubing. They are tailor-made for a variety of modern motorcycles. The heavy duty cast aluminium 15" front wheel has twin discs with fully floating calipers

Heavy duty cast aluminium 15" rear wheel that can be supplied for a large range of modern motorcycles currently in use for side-car duties.

Rhind-Tutt brochure illustrating both touring and sports chairs – plus unique Wasp – developed spaceframe chassis and other details.

Heavy duty cast aluminium 15" side-car wheel and disc brake complete with fully floating Lockheed caliper which is operated from the front master cylinder of the motorcycle

Side-car fittings made to suit most modern motorcycles. The bottom fittings are flanged for greater rigidity.

The unique "Wasp" developed space frame chassis constructed from steel concealed within the glass fibre bodywork is a special feature that gives unparalleled torsional and lateral stability. Also offers passenger impact protection.

sporting single seater to suit most modern motorcycles. Wasp has designed a sub-frame for K-Series BMWs which fits beneath the engine, creating a duplex frame effect and to which the sidecar chassis is rigidly attached by four substantial links.

Bodies are glass fibre, but both models have a space frame of steel tubing concealed within the bodywork and this imparts tremendous torsional and lateral stability and offers some protection for the passengers in the event of a collision.

Other allied products are robust leading link front forks and Y-spoke, 15 inch cast aluminium wheels. Wasp favours car type radials, its choice being mostly S-rated Uniroyals or Michelin 'X' tyres.

Prices are £1808 plus VAT for the child/adult sidecar and £1576 plus VAT for the single seater. Wheels cost £196 plus VAT, while the leading link forks are priced at £380 plus VAT and the cost of suspension units. As a guide, a pair of Bilsteins cost £108 plus VAT.

Addresses of manufacturers and importers:

EML Techniek
Holland bv
Magnoliastraat 20
7161
BW Neede
Holland
Imported by:

E W Pinchbeck & Sons
Over Wallop Coachworks
Nr Stockbridge
Hants
Tel: 0264 781356

Koch Motorrad GmbH
Schlagdstr 31-33
D-3442 Wanfried/Eschwege
West Germany

Unit Sidecars (K Wash)
Wethersfield Road
Sible Hedingham
Nr Halstead
Essex CO9 3LB
Tel: 0787 61000

Vruwink Motor Company
7450 AA Holten
Holland
Postbus 27
Markelesoseweg 17

Wasp Motorcycles
South Newton
Salisbury
Wiltshire
Tel: 0722 743582

14

Specials and Racers

BMW's Compact Drive System with its built-in rear suspension is a 'gift' for 'special' builders, offering as it does a rigid structure on which to hang the front suspension of whatever sort, the fuel tanks and all kinds of bodywork. Given this adaptability without the need for the construction of a conventional steel or aluminium frame or a complicated and expensive fabricated chassis to keep the wheels in their appointed places, it is surprising that there are not more racing, 'street legal' prototypes or specials. But the few that do exist make up for the lack of numbers by their ingenuity.

The four most striking are all prototypes for what may or, indeed, may not become production models. They are the Peraves Oekomobil, the Motorcycle 2000, Krauser's road going version of Rolf Biland's revolutionary Grand Prix sidecar outfit and the Italcaschi Modulo.

The Oekomobil, or Oemil as it's called, from the Swiss Peraves company owned by Arnold Wagner looks very like a long and slender two wheel 'bubble car', but the resemblance ends there as it is capable of 155mph (250km/h). The body is a monocoque of Kevlar and glass fibre bonded with epoxy resin, incorporating internal crash bars. Entrances and exits are effected through a butterfly-type door controlled by a gas strut. The aerodynamic canopy is made of blue-tinted Acrylglass and the makers have employed K100RS mirrors.

Front suspension is by specially stiffened BMW teledraulic forks, separated from the CDS and rear suspension by the air-conditioned passenger compartment which has sound damping carpets, wall insulation and two comfortable upholstered seats in tandem.

Because the bodywork is all-enveloping, neither the rider/driver nor the passenger can touch the ground; take-offs and landings are accomplished with the assistance of an electrically operated undercarriage powered by a K100 starter motor with two small supporting wheels. The undercarriage struts have a manually operated emergency system, just in case, and are semi-automatically retracted by a mechanism actuated by acceleration. The wheels descend in less than half a second and can be left extended up to 30mph (48km/h) to cope with dangerous conditions.

The rear wheel and tyre are standard items, but the front wheel

Oemil from the Swiss Peraves company. This futuristic device, powered by a K100 engine, is capable of 156mph.

has a wider rim and wears a 4.00V18 tyre. A spare wheel is carried transversely, above the CDS, protruding either side and may double as a stabilizing wing. The Oemil is 12ft 3^1/2 inches (3750mm) long, 4ft 10inches (1470mm) high, 2ft 10^1/2inches (880mm) wide and has a wheelbase of 9ft 5inches (2880mm). Fully laden, it weighs 1309lbs (595kg) but will still hit 60mph in 7 seconds. It is far more economical than a standard K100, returning 62.5mpg over 10,000 test kilometres.

Altogether a very different and exciting motorcycle, with a projected price something in the region of £25,000.

The Motorcycle 2000 is the work of Hans Joachim Maier, a design graduate from Southern Germany. With the K100 CDS as a basis, Maier has created a stark but futuristic motorcycle, taking the low seat, foot forward – FF – route to high performance allied to comfort.

Protected by the bodywork in which the fuel tank, instruments, headlight and direction indicators are integrated, the laid-back rider steers through unusual 'introverted' handlebars. Projecting from the fairing, they are connected to a form of hub centre steering with a single drag link. Front suspension is provided by a single unit and two fabricated swinging arms, one above the other on the lefthand, or nearside, of the machine, which pivot from the front end of the engine. There is no frame as such. Everything is mounted on the CDS, while the gearchange lever is mounted on the left hand

handlebar. Handling is expected to be exceptionally good due to the low centre of gravity. The seat is only 17.7 inches (449.5mm) from the ground and the wheelbase is 5ft 6inches (1676mm).

The 2000 was Maier's graduation project at the Phorzhein School of Design and won him top marks from the exam committee. BMW's motorcycle engineers were equally impressed although the company were not involved in any way, other than supplying the parts, and BMW intend to exhibit the machine at motorcycle shows. No performance figures are available, so far.

Krauser's Beo based outfit is known as the Domani, which means 'tomorrow' in Italian. Rolf Biland played a major role in its development but, other than an integrated bodywork covering a chassis rather than a separate bike and sidecar, it bears little real resemblance to the original Beo concept.

The rear wheel and the sidecar wheel of the racing outfit are in line – as in a three-wheeled car – and are driven by a centrally mounted Yamaha engine with chain drive from a gearbox to a complicated cross-shaft with half-shafts either end, while the front wheel of the Beo is offset to the left. The Domani is much more of a conventional outfit. The front wheel and the driven rear wheel are in line with the K100 engine in between and the 'chair' wheel in the usual place. But driver and passenger are side-by-side between the engine and the sidecar wheel, each with a separate cockpit and a separate windscreen, while behind them there is a car-type boot

Motorcycle 2000, the work of Hans Joachim Maier, a design graduate from Southern Germany. Maier used the K100CDS as a basis – with the official blessing of BMW managment.

which will take a lot more luggage than any sidecar boot.

The project is Mike Krauser's special pet and the prototype was built in 1985 with 15 inch wheels and hub centre steering. It weighs 704lbs (320kg) and, with its smooth shape, small frontal area and low C of G, it is very quick, and has incredibly good road holding. The Domani was at the Olympia Motorcycle Show in London in October 1986, and Krauser Imports (UK) Ltd were reported to be interested in selling them at a price somewhere in the region of £10,000. But right hand sidecars are now illegal in Britain and Krausers have no plans to make a left hand version.

Krauser's Beo-based outfit, known as the Domani, still in the development stage.

Only the one prototype exists at present. But a second prototype is currently being built in Switzerland as German legislation prohibits road use of a vehicle without official Type Approval, or Homologation; a Catch 22-like situation which makes it impossible for small volume manufacturers without a test track to road test new designs and virtually rules out small scale production.

The Italaschi Modulo looks very like a high performance version of the Messerschmitt 3-wheeler of three decades ago. It has two small wheels at the front, one small wheel at the back and the driver and the passenger sit one behind the other protected from the weather, if not much else, by a perspex canopy.

The prototype, powered by a complete K75 Compact Drive System, was displayed at the Milan Show in November 1987. It is hoped to offer other power units, including Guzzi, Suzuki, Yamaha and Kawasaki. Dry weight is 704lbs (320kg) and a top speed of 112mph (179km/h) is claimed.

Conventional, road-going, two-wheelers based on K-Series bikes are also pretty rare. The three most notable examples are from Panther-Martin of West Germany the Swiss Egli concern and the Dutch frame builder Nicco Bakker.

The fairing of Panther-Martin's MP1000 – based on the K100 – is said to be aerodynamically efficient, although it is no big deal aesthetically, giving excellent handling, minimum drag and a lower seat height than a standard K. Three-spoke alloy wheels are fitted, with low profile tyres, 110-80 on the front wheel, and 160-60 at the rear. The suspension has been stiffened up and the Martin factory

Dutch frame builder Nicco Bakker's K100 conversion.

offer engine tuning, claiming a top speed of 153mph (245km/h) from the 120bhp unit with a new blue metal silencer.

Nicco Bakker's K100 variation has an all alloy, box-section, mono-shock frame with rear suspension travel of 110mm. Inverted pattern White Power forks with anti-dive are fitted; gold finished, three spoke, cast alloy wheels and a cylindrical gold finished silencer, which is no better looking than the standard item, are also specified. A twin headlamp fairing, single racing seat and boxy tail, a strange, chunky little mudguard extending down the fork legs and a 7 gallon (31.5 litre) petrol tank lend the bike a somewhat brutal, Grand Prix, image. Bakker favours a 16-inch front wheel with a 3.50 section tyre and an 18-inch rear wheel with a 4.50 tyre.

The Egli offering is based upon the K100 engine with power boosted to 118bhp at 9200rpm. Weight is down to 440lbs (200kg) and a top speed of 152mph is claimed. The fuel injection is controlled by a BMW car unit and the inlet valves have been increased in size from 34mm to 36mm. Special cams have been inserted and the K75 pistons raise the compression ratio to 11.4 to 1. The conrods have been lightened by 70gms and a massive 6.16lbs (2.8kg) shaved off the crankshaft. The CDS is suspended, as you might expect, from the now traditional Fritz Egli spine-type frame with Egli forks and White Power shock absorber at the rear.

The road racing scene is by no means overwhelmed by converted K100s and only seven examples spring to mind. There are a brace of bikes built for JJ Automoviles SA of Barcelona, a German roadster/racer being developed by VV Motorradtechnik and four K100RS models raced by Nick Jeffries, Dave Hill, Phil Lovett and several other riders entered by Hughes Motorcycles of Tooting.

Close-up of Nicco Bakker K100 front end showing forks, mudguard and Brembo Gold Line floating calipers.

Original Spanish JJ-Cobas K100R endurance racer. A pair of these machines made their debut at the 1984 Barcelona 24-hour endurance race.

Opposite top: **Braun-BMW K100** racer developed from the JJ-Cobas machines.

Far right: **German VV** Motorradtechnik racer produced 110bhp at 9500rpm and was capable of well over 160mph.

The two Spanish endurance racers were constructed late in 1983 by Antonio Cobas, the internationally renowned chassis expert. Cobas designed a spaceframe, using the Compact Drive System as a stressed member, 40mm Kayaba teledraulic forks and a horizontal monoshock for the standard monolever. Twin floating 300mm Brembo discs with four piston calipers take care of front wheel braking, while the rear wheel has a single Brembo disc with a Brembo caliper. Magnesium three spoke wheels by Marvic, both wearing Michelin race tyres – 16-inch front and 18-inch rear – complete the rolling chassis. The engines were tuned by Eduardo Giro who was Ossa's chief designer at the height of their success. Power output is 122bhp at 9,400rpm, weight is quoted as 394lbs (179kg) and the estimated top speed is in the region of 174mph (278km/h).

Originally campaigned as JJ-Cobas BMW K100RS, the bikes made a poor showing at the 1984 24 Hour Race at Montjuich Park due to problems with the computerized electronic ignition system. But this public humiliation led to assistance from BMW who had previously shown no interest. This in turn, led to sponsorship by

VV racer unveiled, showing unique frame and front forks – note modified fuel injection system and radiator location.

Dave Hill campaigned a basic K100 during the 1984 road racing season, seen here in action at Mallory Park.

Braun, the West German electrical company, through their Spanish subsidiary Braun Española.

From then on the bikes were raced as Braun-BMWs and this timely backing enabled Carlos Cardus to win the 1984 Spanish Superbike Championship. This achievement attracted much publicity at home, but was largely unreported outside Spain.

VV Motorradtechnik specialise in the development and the production of lightweight forks, frames and wheels for BMW's flat twins and have something of a reputation for successful tuning of the 'boxer' engines. They are now developing a high performance K100 for racing or fast road work with their own hub centre steering and a fabricated frame.

Changes to the engine include modifications to the fuel injection and a special 'black box' to control the computerised ignition system. Power output has increased to 110bhp at 9500rpm. Braking is by three 300mm discs from Wiwo, the West German disc brake specialists. Weight of the new VV K100 is given as 370lbs (168kg) and the firm claim a top speed of 155mph (250km/h).

Nick Jefferies, the Yorkshire rider/agent, raced a K100RS in the 1984 and the 1985 Production TT Races in the Isle of Man, on both occasions using bikes with completely standard engines.

He finished 8th in the 1984 event after a non-stop ride, running short of fuel and touring in from the Mountain Box. The bike was very slightly modified with a Koni shock absorber which proved to be inferior to the BMW Nivomat unit. The forks were stiffened up with thicker oil, the footrests were raised, the windscreen aerofoil was taken off and the stands removed, but the mirror/winking indicators were retained.

In September 1988 American Matt Capri, who is behind the Luftmeister range of go-faster goodies, took a K100 turbo charged 'street bike' to an incredible 198.9mph (average 197mph) at the Bonneville speed sessions to claim a new FIM-endorsed world record. This was BMW's first FIM record for 51 years – and faster than any petrol-fuelled bike on the record books, regardless of capacity.

Capri's feat came shortly after fellow American Ken Lyon had steered a Luftmeister tuned K75 turbo streamliner to an average of 182mph – shattering a previous record by nearly 20mph. Maximum velocity attained by the 750 triple was 188mph – compared to the 1000cc record of 183mph in the same streamlined class. Luftmeister plan to reach the tantalising 200mph at the 1989 Bonneville speed session.

Formally service manager with the American BMW importer, Matt Capri has run his tuning business for ten years, working first on the flat twins. A street turbo kit is marketed by Luftmeister aimed at turning the genteel K100 into a beast – the "blower" transforms a mild mannered 90bhp into a snarling 150bhp! But at around £3000 – including a new camshaft and ignition control box to allow higher engine revs, it certainly can't be regarded as cheap.

The 1985 machine was similarly treated, excepting a Nivomat rear shock absorber was fitted and a steering damper cured a tendency to 'tank slappers' on certain sections of the course. A

Nick Jefferies before the start of the 1984 Isle of Man Production TT.

higher axle ratio was tried, but was discarded before the race in which he finished 7th, missing 6th position by 0.6 seconds after lapping at 104mph in wet conditions on his refuelling lap.

Dave Hill, who was sponsored by the Cheylesmore Garage, Coventry, raced a standard K100 in 1984 and was well placed amongst the Japanese mega-bikes in the 500 kilometre race at the West Raynham, Norfolk, circuit.

Phil Lovett was sponsored during 1985 by the now defunct Pineways of Croydon who offered 150 after-market special items for K-Series bikes. Amongst these 'goodies' were new front fork dampers, damper valves and springs, developed by Pineways director Pietro Dimarino to overcome fork dive. These were fitted to the K100RS raced by Lovett which was otherwise a standard bike, although the engine had been stripped and balanced and very carefully put up again.

In practice for the 1985 Production TT it achieved 152mph through the *Motor Cycle News* speed trap, the 5th fastest time recorded in its class, but the bike was never on the leader board. Even more impressive was a 2nd place in the well-supported 6 Hour endurance race at Snetterton a week after the TT. They narrowly missed winning due to Lovett being instructed to ease up when he had an apparently commanding lead. The team and the spectators were convinced that he had won the race when it was announced that he had lost it by 6 seconds. Disappointing as that was, the performance of the bike was very satisfying. It had handled beautifully throughout the race, as it had in the TT, and had used no oil at all so far as anyone could see.

Snetterton 6-hour production race, June 1985.
Pineways-sponsored K100RS ridden by Phil Lovett.

Hughes Motorcycles' racing effort centred on the first K100RS imported into Britain which was used by BMW GB as a press test bike. Hughes bought it at 10,000 miles. They serviced it and entered it for the 500 Kilometre race at West Raynham in 1984. The riders were Ray Knight and Graham Brand who were well placed until the bike was damaged in a pile-up caused by another rider.

The bike was rebuilt and in 1985 it finished 15th overall and 5th in class in a 6 Hour race at Snetterton, ridden once again by Ray Knight and Graham Brand.

1986 Snetterton 6-hour, Hughes Motorcycles of Tooting K100RS (30) with Graham Brand aboard amongst a pack of Oriental megabikes.

In 1986 it was entered for three 6 Hour events at Snetterton. Riders for the first event were Stuart Noon and Graham Brand and, in the later races, Malcolm Hearn and Graham Brand. And on each occasion they were in the prize money with a completely standard engine. After that, the bike retired.

Throughout its racing life the only modifications, apart from Lockheed disc pads and Metzeler Sport tyres, were uprated fork dampers and $1/2$in spacers to pre-load the fork springs. And this was only done to improve the ground clearance, with the rear suspension unit on the stiffest setting.

The bike was also used as a demonstrator and Graham Brand's ride-to-work transport. Everyone who raced it was astonished that it went so well. Graham remarked that a smooth riding style was the best way to the quickest lap times. His only criticism was of rear wheel hopping under heavy braking. Because of this he never used the rear wheel brake.

Appendices

Owners Report by Mick White

The BMW K-Series was launched in 1983 in a blaze of publicity and a fair amount of hype. However it soon became clear through press reports and road tests that the bikes were indeed as good as they were claimed to be. My K100RS is now a year old and having covered 11,000 miles on it from new, I can add my support to the high esteem in which the new BMWs are held.

Before I bought the K100RS I had owned an R65 on which I had travelled some 33,000 miles. At the time of the original announcement of the four-cylinder BMWs I was thinking of trading in the R65, so I arranged a test ride on a standard K100. Half an hour's indulgence convinced me that I ought to save hard and chat up my bank manager in order to buy one; acceleration, handling, low down torque and grin-induceability were all appreciably better than my 650 could manage, yet the extra weight was hardly noticeable. However, I did not like the height of the handlebars and, as I strongly favour a fairing on a large bike to reduce arm and neck ache at speed, waited until the RS was available and bought one. I have not regretted it.

With ascetic dedication I ran the bike in for 3,500 miles. At the time I was regularly riding over 600 miles per week, so it did not take long to complete my breaking-in programme. I even managed 65mpg in the early low-revving days. Oil consumption at first was noticeable – say $1/2$ pint per 1,000 – but as carbon build up around the circumference of the piston crowns consumption diminished and is now nil.

One of the first trips I made was a late-night journey from London to Bristol, using the A4. I was immediately disappointed with the power and spread of light from the headlamp, especially in view of the fact that the standard K100 headlamp had received a good press and certainly my old R65 was no glow worm; indeed, all had 60-watt halogen bulbs. I decided that the rectangular shape of the reflector on the RS was to blame so I fitted a 100/80 watt bulb which certainly brightened things up; I have since replaced it with a 130/90 watt bulb which is superb and, do not worry, it has not melted the reflector or caused the generator any problems so far.

I have fitted BMW panniers and, although the carrying frames look a bit like the Shell Oil logo, they hold the panniers much more rigidly than the rectangular frames did on the R65. I never had

The First 11,000 miles of K100RS Ownership – Mick White August 1985

serious problems with the R65's frames but the security of the K100 attachment gives me more peace of mind. Also, the panniers do not cause the bike to weave at speed; the R65's panniers used to take control at speeds in excess of 85mph. The small tote bag which straps to the rear carrier is useful but is a nuisance to fit and remove; yet if you leave it on the bike its contents cannot be secured against theft.

Faults have been very few. The bike was officially recalled twice – once for a revised rear brake master cylinder and again for an earth-wiring modification to the right thumb control pad on the handlebar, neither of which had given me any trouble but the original brake cylinder can apparently be damaged by journalists who ride into the sea. The electronic speedo ceased to function after about 3,500 miles, just as I took the bike up to maximum speed in top for the first and only time so far. I did not get the satisfaction of seeing some 135mph on the clock but I did see peak revs (8,250rpm) on the rev counter. The speedo was repaired under guarantee.

Other minor faults have been a starter motor which sometimes fails to engage, necessitating a bump-start on a couple of occasions; slight oil mist at certain engine cover bolts; a failed rear stoplight switch, replaced under guarantee; and a petrol cap which harbours rainwater which then proceeds straight into the tank when you open the cap – the trick is to be ready with a fistful of garage forecourt absorbent paper with which you stem the tide before it gets a chance to contaminate the 4-star. However, I understand that the bike is to be recalled again for a modification to the fuel cap.

I have also had some bad luck with rear wheel punctures, although that is not the bike's fault. I collected a 2" floorboard nail after a couple of thousand miles and, although the tubeless Metzler deflated very slowly and I got home safely, the tyre was beyond repair. Having bought another brand new Metzler, would you believe that within a fortnight I picked up a 2" woodscrew! Again I got home safely but, rather than spend yet another £40 or more on a tyre, I patched the inside of the damaged cover and fitted a tube. That was safe enough during the winter months but a new set of tubeless covers have been fitted since. At least the punctures taught me that tubeless tyres do not deflate quickly even though it is easy to damage them beyond repair and the rear wheel of a K100 is swiftly and easily removed and replaced.

The brake pads eventually wore out and I was seduced by a Ferodo salesman at the 1984 Olympic Show into buying his product as used by Joey Dunlop etc. The new front pads fitted well and perform neither better nor worse than the original BMW pads except that they squeal a bit less and cost a lot less. The rear pads, however, were a real tight fit lengthways and, after a few pumps on the brake pedal, they jammed solid. Being short of time, I had to take the whole bike to the dealer's for them to free the pads and be soundly chastised for departing from the use of genuine BMW spares. I ruefully sent the offending pads and the dealer's bill to Ferodo for reimbursement. I received a reply which admitted that the pads were oversize and enclosing a cheque for the full amount plus two complimentary sets of pads. Thanks, Ferodo.

Despite our wet climate, I have had no problems of water ingress anywhere (except via the petrol cap). All the idiot lights still work, as does the quartz clock which I find extremely useful and which, with typical Bavarian efficiency, is accurate to within 5 seconds a month!

Basic maintenance is easy. I did both the 5,000 and 10,000 miles services myself apart from adjusting the fuel injectors and the valve clearances (by shims), which I entrusted to the dealer. Oil changes are straightforward and the engine oil filter is of the screw-on canister type but with a subtle difference; it has a 17mm hexagon glued on the end making removal simplicity itself. Hands up anyone who has, like me, spent all day trying to unscrew, with zero hand-room and leverage, the oil filter on a Ford Fiesta? I also changed the fuel filter (which is actually inside the tank) with no problems. Changing the front fork fluid is also straightforward, if a little fiddly, but I have made a slight improvement in the fork action by replacing the original 5-weight fluid with Castrol 15W/30 fork oil; naturally the forks still dip sharply under heavy braking (and in my opinion need some form of anti-dive or at least stiffer springs) but the lazier damping caused by the thicker oil has given the front-end a bit more controllability.

Incidentally, do not believe anyone who tells you that the petrol tank holds 4.8 gallons. There is so much gubbins inside the tank (filter, fuel pump, yards of tubing) that actually capacity is a fraction under four gallons. Also, if you fill the tank to anywhere near the brim, the infamous cap will leak, depositing a stain down the left side of the tank – despite the presence of an overflow pipe. There is slight high-frequency vibration to be felt through the handlebar at around 3,500 revs which can be annoying in town when the engine is often operating at that speed. I cured it quite fortuitously by fitting heated grips which, being slightly fatter than the standard rubbers, dampen out the vibes. Fitting Grab-Ons would no doubt also do the job. The BMW heated grips work very well and give two heat ratings; medium rare and well done. They also wire straight into sockets in the main harness with no home-made joining or soldering, but you do have to drill the handlebar for the cable routing.

The K100RS lends itself naturally to long trips and motorcycling holidays. It is the sort of bike with which a rider can confidently tackle John O' Groats to Lands End or the Beaujolais Run. A visit to last year's TT was completed without a hitch and the luggage capacity ensured that I was able to take with me everything I needed and more, room for a bottle of Glen Kella Manx Whiskey and half a stone of Devereux's kippers on the return journey.

At this point I must include a plug for the dealer I have mentioned a couple of times, but firstly a cautionary tale. I bought my R65 new, at a discount, from a Tesco-type establishment which shall be nameless, but it was a dreadful mistake. That company, I soon realised, had no idea about BMWs, carried few spare parts and had no BMW agency. I even unwittingly invalidated the bike's guarantee by doing the first service myself rather than return the bike to the firm's workshop which, by failing to carry out any kind of PDI, had proved its inefficiency at the outset. Instead I started buying my spares from Hughes Motorcycles of Tooting, London, and found here a small knowledgeable and enthusiastic dealer of traditional virtues. I subsequently bought my K100RS from Hughes, receiving a fair trade-in on the well-used R65 and have always obtained prompt, efficient service from them and have been freely offered advice. I would not entrust a K100 for repair or service to anyone other than an established enfranchised dealer such as Hughes in servicing and maintenance.

Without question the K100 and its derivatives are very expensive bikes to buy new. I am now satisfied, however, that a well-kept secondhand version with 10,000 miles or more under its wheels is a sound investment and at a significantly lower outlay. Just as important is the fact that reliability and long service intervals make a 'K' comparatively cheap to run. I hope to be able to report in a year's time that even at 20,000 plus miles, a K100 is still, like the boxer twins, well worth buying.

50,000 miles on a K100RS – An owner's report – Mick White, October 1987

The K100RS that was the subject of my article in the August 1985 issue of *Motorcycle Enthusiast* has now covered over 50,000 miles in 3 years 9 months of ownership since being purchased new in January 1984. I had originally intended to follow the article up with a 25,000 mile report, but the bike had been so boringly reliable that there was nothing of any substance to say about it. Now, however, I feel that A588 SGO has earned its wings and deserves another mention.

The bike has been used mostly for daily commuting between Essex and London, but has enjoyed one or two more stimulating excursions. It has been to the Isle of Man twice, on two European holidays (two-up), several trips to Scotland and Wales, two National Rallies and sundry visits to NEC Shows, race meetings, far-flung autojumbles etc. It has never failed to complete a journey.

More often than not I ride the 'K' hard and on the IOM trips and on one of the holidays abroad I was accompanied by a friend on a newer and faster Kawasaki GPZ900R, resulting in rapid rear tyre wear and frequent fuel stops. The most graphic illustration of such an exploit that I can give concerned a ride to an airport, along with the Kawasaki, to catch a plane. It happened in mid 1987 when the BMW had about 45,000 on the clock (and was due for a service to boot). We had set out in what we thought was plenty of time but were beset by roadworks, lorries and red traffic lights and, with about 60 miles to go, we had only a little over 30 minutes before the plane took off and the Kwacker needed to stop for petrol! Never have I ridden a road bike so fast for so long; with full panniers, a tank bag and a well-laden luggage rack, the "Flying Brick" covered over 50 miles of autobahn at 8000rpm, a speedo reading of 135mph. At that speed the bike was rock steady and the fairing kept the rider well out of the airstream. We caught the plane. When I returned three days later, I found that the bike had been standing out in virtually continuous rain, yet it started immediately and showed no sign of having endured such a thrashing. In fairness, neither did the Kwacker, but this is a book about BMWs!

I have made a few modifications to the bike. Firstly I replaced the original brake fluid lines with Aeroquip hoses, though I must admit I noticed no difference in "feel" afterwards. They do look good, though. The dualseat has gone in favour of an Italian Giuliari item with a removable hump; this was mainly because I always found the seat height a bit high and the Giuliari is lower but, again, I think it looks good. The front fork springs were always, in my opinion, a bit soft and after a bit of experimentation Hughes Motorcycles of Tooting have managed to fit the later Mk II fork springs, which together with 30-weight fork oil has firmed up the front-end a treat; a further planned mod is to fit a Spax rear shock to harden the rear suspension. I junked the square silencer for a Motad, which fits straight on with no alterations necessary to the fuel injection, is no louder and which is aesthetically 10 times better; I have not noticed any increase or decrease in performance as a result. Finally, I substituted a Krauser rear carrier for the BMW version as it gives a flat, horizontal platform for luggage and accommodates bungee straps more easily.

Another epic ride took place in April 1986 when I made a journey between Wolverhampton and Aberdeen, a trip of 400-odd miles that I had done many times in my youth when I was a student. The first attempt, at the tender age of 17, had been done in 12 hours on a Ducati Daytona. This had been improved to 9 hours on a BSA A7 over the next 3 years. With the benefit of more motorways and several new bypasses around small towns on the A9 and A94, the BMW did the journey in 5 hours 40 minutes.

A final anecdote on the KRS's ability to hurry along begins after a heavy assault on a large quantity of Belgian beer perpetrated by a friend and me in Antwerp on the last night of a European tour. Having slept through our alarms at 9am, we woke devastatingly hungover at 10.30am with the vague realisation that we were due in Calais to catch a hovercraft in the very near future. What should have been a leisurely canter turned into a panic-laden sprint to the French port. But the bike took the two-up dash in its stride and we made it in time, despite my shaky hands and bloodshot vision.

BMWs are expected to be reliable and, indeed, should be for the price and mine is no exception. There are, however, some minor problems which I believe are common to most of the K-Series. Some of the faults, or potential faults, were corrected on my bike by recall at no charge, namely the rear brake master cylinder, handlebar switch earth wire, fuel cap, ignition black box, fuel pump and re-routed throttle cable; only the leaky fuel cap had caused me problems. The rear brake light switch wire lives down by the brake pedal and enjoys constant abuse from rain, grit, salt etc, often fails and can blow a fuse which also protects the instrument lights and heated handlebar grips; they will not come on again until the brake switch is unplugged from the wiring harness and the fuse replaced. An idiot light tells you that the switch has failed, usually before the fuse blows. Frequent squirts of WD40 will delay failure, but the switch is clearly a poor design and ought to have been corrected by BMW. I am on my 4th or 5th switch at present and expect to have to buy a 6th soon. The front brake light switch has also had to be replaced once.

The screen spoiler broke away from its fixing screws at 15,500 miles and was so flimsily mounted that I have not bothered to fit a new one because it would surely break again; turbulence is slightly increased as a result although the spoiler was only really effective at over 90mph. A backfire sometimes causes embarrassment on the overrun and is possibly the result of a hiccup in the fuel cut-out device which cancels out at 2,000 revs. At 22,000 miles I had to fit a new throttle cable as a strand had broken in the original; fitting the new one was an extremely fiddly job as it has to be threaded through some restricted gaps and connected blind to the injector pulley. The cable cost a cool £9! At 37,300 miles the headlamp bulb deflector disc fell off and I had to replace the complete reflector assembly (although I did manage to buy a second-hand one). While I had the fairing apart I gave the metal inner panels a coat of Hammerite, a treatment I also gave to the rear sub-frame tubes when I fitted the new seat; these hidden metal components are prone to rusting if left too long to their own devices. The clutch cable was replaced at 40,000 miles. Two bulbs have blown. And finally, I have had quite bad oil leaks from the alternator cover and have had the gasket replaced twice.

Whilst the above catalogue of gripes reflects none too well on the Ks in general, I must also give the other side of the equation. The following items of original equipment are still giving excellent service and might well have been replaced by now on other makes: clutch, cam chain, steering bearings, wheel bearings, all engine components, brake discs, fuel pump, starter motor, electrics, electronics, battery, fork seals, even footrest rubbers! The clutch has been adjusted only three times, which considering the many thousands of miles of congested roads the bike has travelled, is testament indeed to its durability.

Maintenance has been carried out scrupulously according to the handbook, though I have changed the engine oil (Duckhams Hypergrade) at 2,500 mile intervals rather than the recommended 5,000 miles. No oil needs to be added between changes. The fuel filter has been replaced at 10,000 mile intervals (20,000 recommended) and the coolant every 10,000 miles (instead of annually – I cover more than 10,000 miles per year). I always mix the antifreeze with distilled water as I live in a hard water area and I do not want the alloy engine to silt up. Sparking plugs generally last a bit less than the 10,000 miles suggested in the handbook and I now replace them routinely at 5,000 miles; Bosch K5DC plugs are perfectly satisfactory but I have also tried ND X24ES-U with good results.

Hughes Motorcycles of Tooting, London (highly recommended) has always handled the things I cannot do; valve clearances and CO emissions. Everything else is within the scope of the average home mechanic. It would help, though, if BMW or someone would produce a workshop manual. Eventually the engine will need surgery and it is not so esoteric that a competent amateur cannot handle, say, a change of piston rings or big-end bearings, given a manual to refer to.

Having ridden the bike for such a distance, I have naturally grown to like and dislike some of its features and characteristics.

Its plusses are its reliability, speed, comfort, luggage capacity and its ability as an all-rounder. You can ride it to the chip shop and back, commute to work with your Filofax in the seat storage compartment, or ride it overland to Australia and it will do all of these things perfectly well. It is also easy to maintain.

I have already mentioned some of the minuses: softish suspension, ugly silencer, highish seat. Another front fork nuisance is a rattle going over bumps. I also have reservations about the brakes, which I find adequate without being startling: cast iron discs and, perhaps, AP Lockheed calipers would in my opinion be an improvement, having found them excellent on other makes of bike. The petrol tank also needs a bigger capacity as at present, ridden hard, fill-ups are needed every 140 miles or so which is too frequent for a touring machine. The headlamp needs a more powerful bulb. The gearchange, though better than that on the boxer twins, is still chunky and seems to have worsened as the miles have built up. The starter motor sometimes fails to engage first time.

The suspension has been stiffened up on the 'Mk II' bikes. The future MK III version will, I hope, incorporate the improvements I have suggested.

However, I am still committed to my K100. Before owning it, I was always ready to change my bike every couple of years (and in some cases, every 6 months!), and road tests in magazines were always scanned diligently and different machines compared. Since I bought the Brick, I have not seriously considered changing it for any other model, though I have had a sneaky test ride on a F1 Ducati for the hell of it. But it was just a brief, extra-marital fling, fun at the time but not the stuff of long-term relationships!

The KRS has worked its way through several sets of tyres and brake pads and has given me the opportunity to compare different brands and wear rates. It is, however, difficult to be specific about tyre life as I went through a really bad period of punctures: *thirteen* in a year! At first I was replacing each tyre as soon as it was punctured but this naturally became extremely expensive and eventually I resorted to either plugging the tubeless cover or inserting an inner tube. The tyres involved were Metzlers ME99s, Dunlop K391s and Pirelli Phantoms (all rear except one Pirelli front) and all were satisfactory in terms of grip. All, however, reacted badly to raised white lines in the road. One or two of these tyres died a natural death rather than by a nail through the heart; one rear K391 lasted 8,500 miles and one Pirelli front nearly 17,000 miles. I fitted Michelin Hi-Sports at 47,000 miles and they are still on the bike. The Michelins are the best of the bunch, giving good grip, especially in the wet, and not reacting so violently to road surface irregularities, but they are wearing out quite quickly. You do have to be assertive in cornering, however, because if you wally round a bend the bike will tip into the corner. Pretend you are Ronnie Haslam and you will be all right. The other slight problem with the Hi-Sports is that they are not made in the recommended K100 sizes of 100/90V18 front and

130/90V17 rear; I fitted 100/80V18 front and 140/70V17 rear which lower the bike a fraction and call for a Bullworker course to heave it onto the centre stand, and which cause the speedometer to give readings that are 6% or 7% optimistic. In retrospect I think a 110/80V18 would be a better proposition on the front to lessen the width ratio between front and rear tyres. I intend to stick with Michelins for the foreseeable future, hopefully finding radials in suitable sizes next time. After all this tyre swapping, I am now on first name terms with the fitters at the local tyre depot!

Brake pads are easier to compare. The original equipment lasted 10,000 miles, worked reasonably well but the front pads squealed in operation. I replaced the fronts with Ferodo FDB 148 pads which did not squeal but performed identically. The Ferodos lasted another 10,000 miles, being replaced with more Ferodos which lasted another 10,000 miles and tended to break up rather than wear down. At 40,000 miles I fitted EBC FA18 (M323GG compound) which are probably the best of the lot, having good performance and wearing well. Rear pads have been replaced more frequently, evidently because of all the crawling through London traffic that I do, balancing throttle, clutch and rear brake for mile after mile. After the first 10,000 miles I fitted Lockheed LMP 127 pads that in turn had to be replaced at 15,500 miles with BMW pads. At 24,000 miles I substituted EBC FA18 (249GG compound), likewise at 33,500 miles, which wore out after a further 6,500 miles when I fitted AP Lockheed LMP 106 asbestos-free pads which are due for replacement now (at 50,600 miles). All of these pads have been similar in performance, with the EBCs having the edge, especially in the wet, but I still believe that stainless steel is inferior to cast iron for the discs and that the brakes would be significantly better if so equipped. I intend to try SBS or Dunlopads next.

After nearly four years of virtually daily use, summer and winter, some deterioration of a machine's paintwork, alloy castings etc may be expected. Each year I have treated the fairing and body panels to a coating of Simoniz Resin Glaze, followed up by frequent washes and wax polishes, with the result that the paintwork (metallic blue) retains a bright appearance. The fairing does however bear the scars of stone chips thrown up by a million Volvo rear tyres but the bike has never been dropped and so there is no serious body damage. One of these days I may give the bike a complete respray in my favourite Italian racing red (turning it into a *red brick!*). The engine castings and other alloy parts have been sprayed in the winter with a BMW aerosol wax concoction called Transparent-Wachs, with the result that no salt damage has occurred. As I mentioned earlier, out-of-sight steel components can start to rust if not protected (inner fairing panels, rear sub-frame tubing, seat pan and fixings). The fibre mudguards are a boon and require no maintenance other than cleaning. The chromework (virtually just the fork stanchions) has no rust but the stainless exhaust system is hard to clean and is permanently discoloured. The stainless brake discs are scored but not so badly as to warrant skimming or replacement yet. Even the centre and side stands have not rusted.

Overall, then, the Ks have a durable, quality finish that, given a bit of tender loving care, will retain a showroom appearance and even win the odd *concours d'élégance* if the owner is dedicated enough.

The Ks have broken the mould of the long line of BMW Boxers and have proved themselves to be worthy of the marque. I have often heard the more conservative of BMW enthusiasts expressing fear and loathing about the intrusion of these water-cooled upstarts into such a proud heritage.

I have owned three BMWs in my motorcycling career. The first was a 1959 R69, purchased second-hand in 1968 and kept for over 5 years. On it I had a memorable holiday in Yugoslavia with no problems other than a brief loss of sparks owing to torrential rain in the Istrian mountains. That bike was the smoothest BMW I have ever ridden (in fact the smoothest motorcycle I have ever ridden), was extremely long-legged and comfortable, and permitted very high cruising speeds in comparison to its contemporary British vertical twins. I bought it from a Scotsman who described it as a "bike and a half"; how right he was. I had a lot of travelling to do in my job in those days and used the R69 in preference to an official car.

Prior to buying the K100RS I had a new R65 which covered an indecently high mileage in a very short space of time, thanks to a 90-mile daily commuting journey, weekend visits to see my girlfriend (now my wife) who lived 190 miles away, and all sorts of other trips. It was an extremely nimble machine, utterly reliable (a worn-through electrical wire and a dislodged choke cable were my only problems) and very pretty, but it struggled to maintain really high cruising speeds. I would have loved to have squirted that bike round the Brands short circuit, so enthusiastic was it to go round corners.

The K100 has become the best bike I have owned in 25 years of motorcycling. Compared to its forefathers it lacks the smoothness of the Earles fork twins, is not so cheeky round tight corners as the smaller modern Boxers, and other makes have scored over it in specific areas. Certainly it lacks the sheer speed and acceleration of the specious products from the Japanese manufacturers.

But overall it has in my opinion no equal. It is a BMW in every sense.

So what do you do with a 50,000 mile BMW? Do another 50,000 on it, of course. It has always been my long-term aim to cover 100,000 miles on the KRS before making any decisions on its future. After all, the odometer's limit is 999,999!

Next year the six-points run is planned as a sponsored charity ride (ie the four extremities of the British mainland plus John O' Groats and Land's End). A tour of Ireland, spectating at some road races, also beckons. Not forgetting many more thousands of miles going to work and back.

I do not anticipate having any major work done on the engine before the 100,000 mark is reached. I can only compare that comment with my experience with another bike (not a BMW) that I owned a number of years ago and which also had done a high mileage; that was by no means a bad machine but in 52,000 miles it had had a rebore and pistons, new big-end shells and four lots of valve springs (complete with seat cutting and valve grinding).

I think I can best sum up ownership of a K-Series BMW in the word *confidence.* Given correct maintenance, there is no reason why any K should not give years of service in all conditions and for all purposes. I think I have proved it.

APPENDIX TWO

Special Equipment (ex factory)

	K100	K100RS	K100RT	K100LT	Special equipment retro-fittable
ABS$_1$	x	x	x	x	-
Temperature and fuel gauge	-	x	x	x	XX
Hazard warning flashers	x	x	x	o	XX
Digital clock	x	o	o	o	XX
Dual-tone fanfare	x	o	o	o	XX
Socket	x	x	x	o	XX
Additional socket	-	-	x	o	XX
Heatable grips	x	x	x	-	XX
Anti-theft alarm	x	x	x	x	XX
Low handlebar	x	-	-	-	XX
High seat (80mm/31.5in) with grab strap	.	-	-	-	XX
without grab strap	.	-	-	-	XX
Splashguard at rear	x	x	x	x	XX
Longer splashguard at rear	-	-	-	x	XX
Solo seat	-	x	-	-	XX
Engine protection bars	x	x	x	x	XX
Engine spoiler	-	x	-	-	XX
Side-stand, automatic	x	x	x	x	XX
Windshield (with 800mm seat only)	x	-	-	-	XX
Self-levelling	x	x	x	o	XX
Sports suspension	-	x	-	-	-
Low windshield (430mm/16.9in)$_4$	-	-	-	x	XX
High windshield (560mm/22.0in)$_5$	-	-	-	x	XX
High windshield with side flaps	-	-	-	x	XX
Additional instrument panel with low and high windshield	-	-	-	x	XX
Luggage rack	x	x	x	o	XX
Set of integral cases with supports	x	x	o	o	XX
Set of city cases with supports	x	x	-	-	XX
Topcase, small$_2$	x	x	x	o	XX
Topcase, large$_2$	-	-	-	x	XX
Knee-padding	-	x	x	x	XX
Radio installation kit	-	-	x	o	XX
Radio suppressor	-	-	x	o	XX
Fresh-air duct fork opening	-	.	.	.	-
Exhaust spoiler	-	-	x	x	XX
Super toolkit	x	x	x	x	XX$_2$
First-aid kit	x	x	x	x	XX

	K75	K75C	K75S	Special equipment retro-fittable
Luggage rack	x	x	x	xx
Set of integral cases with supports	x	x	x	xx
Set of city cases with supports	x	x	x	xx
Topcase, small$_2$	x	x	x	xx
Knee-padding	-	x	x	xx
Super toolkit	x	x	x	xx$_3$
First-aid kit	x	x	x	xx
Hazard warning flashers	x	x	x	xx
Digital clock	x	x	o	xx
Dual-tone fanfare	-	x	x	xx
Socket	x	x	x	xx
Heatable grips	x	x	x	xx
Anti-theft alarm	x	x	x	xx
High handlebar	x	x	-	xx
Splashguardat rear	x	x	x	xx
High-comfort seat	-	x	-	xx
High seat (800mm/31.5in) with grab strap	.	-	-	xx
without grab strap	.	-	-	xx
Solo seat in red or black	-	x	x	xx
Engine protection bars	x	x	-	xx
Engine spoiler	-	x	o	xx
Side-stand, automatic	x	x	x	xx
Windshield instead of cockpit fairing	-	.	-	-
High-comfort suspension	o	o	.	-
Sports suspension	-	-	o	-
Self-levelling	x	x	-$_6$	xx

x = available as special equipment ex factory
xx = available as retrofittable special equipment
- = not available
o = standard
. = optional at no extra charge

$_1$ = only in conjunction with high-comfort suspension
$_2$ = only in conjunction with luggage rack
$_3$ = supplementary toolkit
$_4$ = in the Federal Republic of Germany only
$_5$ = not allowed in the Federal Republic of Germany
$_6$ = from Spring 1988

Other special equipment for all K75 and K100 models

Soft rubber handlebar grips (standard on the K100LT; not available with heatable grips)
Wind deflector (K100 only)
Cockpit fairing (K100 only)
Additional headlight (K100 only)
Luggage roll
Multivario K tank bag
Citybag

APPENDIX THREE

Factory Specifications

	SPECIFICATIONS		K 75 and K 75 C	K 75 S		
Engine	Cubic capacity	cc	740	740		
	Bore/stroke	mm	67/70	67/70		
	Max output	kW/bhp	55/75	55/75		
	at	rpm	8500	8500		
	Max torque	Nm	68	68		
	at	rpm	6750	6750		
	Design		inline	inline		
	No of cylinders		3	3		
	Compression ratio/fuel grade (also unleaded)		11.0 S	11.0 S		
	Valve control		DOHC	DOHC		
	Valves per cylinder		2	2		
	Intake/outlet dia	mm	34/30	34/30		
	Fuel supply		LE-Jetronic with coasting cut-off			
Electrical system	Ignition		VZ-51 L digital ignition			
	Alternator	W	460	460		
	Battery	V/Ah	12/25	12/25		
	Headlight	W	H 4 55/60	H 4 55/60		
	Starter	kW	0.7	0.7		
Power transmission, Gearbox	Gearbox		5-speed gearbox with dog-type shift			
	Gear ratios	I	4.50/3.20	4.50/3.20		
		II	2.96/3.20	2.96/3.20		
		III	2.30/3.20	2.30/3.20		
		IV	1.88/3.20	1.88/3.20		
		V	1.67/3.20	1.67/3.20		
Suspension	Rear-wheel drive		Encapsulated drive shaft with universal joint and integrated torsion damper			
	Clutch		Single-plate dry clutch rotating in opposite direction			
	Type of frame		Tubular space frame, engine serving as loadbearing component			
	Spring travel front/rear	mm	185/110	135/110		
	Wheel castor	mm	101	101		
	Wheelbase	mm	1516	1516		
	Brakes (asbestos-free)	Front:	dual-disc brake, dia 285 mm			
		Rear:	drum brake, dia 200 mm	single-disc brake, dia 285 mm		
	Wheels	front	Light-alloy wheels 2.50 – 18 MTH 2	Light-alloy wheels 2.50 – 18 MTH 2		
		rear	2.75 – 18 MTH 2	2.75 – 17 MTH 2		
	Tyres	front	100/90/H 18	100/90/V 18		
		rear	120/90/H 18 tubeless	130/90/V 17 tubeless		
Dimensions and weights	Length, overall	mm	2220	2220		
	Width with mirrors	mm	900	810		
	Handlebar width without mirrors	mm	710	650		
	Seat height	mm	760*	810		
	Weight, unladen with full tank	kg	228	235		
	Max permissible weight	kg	450	450		
	Fuel tank	ltr	21	21		
Performance	Fuel consumption					
	90 km/h (56 mph)	ltr	4.5	4.3		
	110 km/h (68 mph)	ltr	5.2	5.0		
	Acceleration					
	0–100 km/h (62 mph)	sec	4.6	4.6		
	standing-start km	sec	25.6	25.2		
	Top speed	km/h	200	210		
Model features	Fairing		K 75 C only: glass-fibre-reinforced plastic cockpit fairing fitted to handlebar or high windshield	Glass-fibre-reinforced plastic sports fairing fitted to frame, glass-fibre-reinforced engine spoiler		
	Standard features		Repair kit, toolkit	Repair kit, toolkit, digital clock		

* K 75 C: 810

	SPECIFICATIONS		K 100	K 100 RS	K 100 RT and K 100 LT	K 1
Engine	Cubic capacity	cc	987	987	987	987
	Bore/stroke	mm	67/70	67/70	67/70	67/70
	Max output	kW/bhp	66/90	66/90	66/90	74/100
	at	rpm	8000	8000	8000	8000
	Max torque	Nm	86	86	86	100
	at	rpm	6000	6000	6000	6750
	Design		inline	inline	inline	inline
	No of cylinders		4	4	4	4
	Compression ratio/fuel grade (also unleaded)		10.2 N	10.2 N	10.2 N	11.0 S
	Valve control		DOHC	DOHC	DOHC	DOHC
	Valves per cylinder		2	2	2	4
	Intake/outlet dia	mm	34/28	34/28	34/28	26,5/23
	Fuel supply		LE-Jetronic	LE-Jetronic	LE-Jetronic	Motronic
Electrical system	Ignition		VZ-51 L digital ignition			Motronic
	Alternator	W	460	460	460	460
	Battery	V/Ah	12/25	12/25	12/25	12/25
	Headlight	W	H 4 55/60	H 4 55/60	H 4 55/60	H 4 55/60
	Starter	kW	0.7	0.7	0.7	0.7
Power transmission, Gearbox	Gearbox		5-speed gearbox with dog-type shift			
	Gear ratios	I	4.50/2.91	4.50/2.81	4.50/2.91	4.50/2.75
		II	2.96/2.91	2.96/2.91	2.96/2.91	2.96/2.75
		III	2.30/2.91	2.30/2.81	2.30/2.91	2.30/2.75
		IV	1.88/2.91	1.88/2.81	1.88/2.91	1.88/2.75
		V	1.67/2.91	1.67/2.81	1.67/2.91	1.61/2.75
Suspension	Rear-wheel drive		Encapsulated drive shaft with universal joint and integrated torsion damper			BMW Paralever
	Clutch		Single-plate dry clutch rotating in opposite direction, dia 180 mm			
	Type of frame		Tubular space frame, engine serving as load-bearing component			
	Spring travel front/rear	mm	185/110	185/110	185/110	135/140
	Wheel castor	mm	101	101	101	90
	Wheelbase	mm	1516	1516	1516	1560
	Brakes	Front:	dual-disc fixed-calliper brake, dia 285 mm			Ø 305 mm
		Rear:	integrated fixed-calliper disc brake, dia 285 mm			Ø 285 mm
	Wheels		Light-alloy wheels	Light-alloy wheels	Light-alloy wheels	LM
		front	2.50 – 18 MTH 2	2.50 – 18 MTH 2	2.50 – 18 MTH 2	3.50 - 17 MTH 2
		rear	2.75 – 17 MTH 2	2.75 – 17 MTH 2	2.75 – 17 MTH 2	4.50 - 18 MTH 2
	Tyres	front	100/90 V 18	100/90 V 18	100/90 V 18	120/70-VR 17
		rear	130/90 V 17	130/90 V 17	130/90 V 17	160/60-VR 18
			tubeless	tubeless	tubeless	tubeless
Dimensions and weights	Length, overall	mm	2220	2220	2220	2250
	Width with mirrors	mm	960	800	916	760
	Handlebar width	mm	755	690	770	670
	Seat height	mm	760	810	810	780
	Weight, unladen with full tank	kg	240	253	263	258
	Max permissible weight	kg	480	480	480	480
	Fuel tank	ltr	21	22	22	22
Performance	Fuel consumption 90 km/h (56 mph)	ltr	5.0	4.3	4.4	
	110 km/h (68 mph)	ltr	5.7	5.1	5.4	
	Acceleration 0–100 km/h (62 mph)	sec	4.0	4.0	4.1	
	standing-start km	sec	23.6	23.5	24.1	
	Top speed	km/h	215	220	215	more than 230
Model features	Fairing			Multi-piece aerodynamically optimized sports fairing (glass-fibre-reinforced plastic)	Multi-piece aerodynamically optimized touring fairing (glass-fibre-reinforced plastic)	Multi-piece aerodynamically optimized sports fairing
	Standard features			Repair kit, toolkit, digital clock	Repair kit, toolkit, digital clock, high handlebar, integral cases with support and standard key	Repair kit, toolkit digital clock Central locking
					Additional K 100 LT features: hazard warning flashers, radio installation kit, radio suppression, 30 Ah battery, 2 sockets, soft rubber handlebars, high-comfort seat, self-levelling, luggage rack, topcase	

APPENDIX FOUR

UK Prices

UK RECOMMENDED RETAIL PRICES OF ALL K-SERIES STANDARD MODELS FROM OCTOBER 1983

	Launch	April'84 on	Mar.'85 on	Feb.'86 on	Jan.'87 on	Jun.'87 on	Jan.'88 on
K75C	£3750			£3825	£4115	£4238	£4450
K75S	£4131				£4553	£4689	£5035
K75	£3966				£3966	£4055	£4150
K75SS	£4783				£4783	£4926	Discont.
K100	£3290	£3490	£3725	£3914	£4423	£4556	£4870
K100RS	£4290	£4390	£4650	£4886	£5395	£5519	£5685
K100RT	£4490	£4595	£4750	£4988	£5507	£5629	£5800
K100LT	£5855				£5855	£6031	£6319

APPENDIX FIVE

UK Factory Appointed Dealers

There are some sixty-five BMW motorcycle dealers throughout the British Isles and the consensus of opinion amongst the sixty-five is that twenty-five would be enough. But, assuming that BMW would agree to a reduction, it would be a lengthy process due to long-term contracts.

The dealers have a point, although you could be excused for thinking that their attitude is based entirely on self-interest and is, therefore, quite predictable. But the hard commercial fact is that approximately 2000 BMWs, both K-Series and 'boxers', will be sold this year in the United Kingdom. An average of only 30.76 machines per dealer, from which you can deduce that the majority of dealers are not likely to become 'fat cats' and a reduction in the dealer network might be desirable from everybody's point of view. On the other hand, owners might be better served by the authorisation of more servicing points and spares outlets.

AVON
Wellsway Motors
Bath (0225) 29187/8

BERKSHIRE
Vincents of Reading
Reading (0734)866161

BUCKINGHAMSHIRE
Gardner and White Limited
Stoke Goldington
Milton Keynes (090 855) 469
SGT Superbiking
Taplow Burnham (06286) 5353

CAMBRIDGESHIRE
Andy Lee
Cambridge (0223) 249251
W.H. Balderston
Peterborough (0733) 65470

CLEVELAND
Armstrong Motorcycles
Middlesbrough (0642) 818007

CORNWALL
Keith Parnell Motorcycles Limited
Redruth (0209) 821045

CUMBRIA
John Stewart Motorcycles
Barrow in Furness (0229) 24757

DERBYSHIRE
Roy Pidcock Motorcycles Limited
Derby (0332) 49673/367947

DEVON
SMB (Exeter) Limited
Exeter (0392) 69595

DORSET
CW Motorcycles
Dorchester (0305) 69370

ESSEX
Fairfield Superbikes Limited
Leigh on Sea (0702) 715911
Ongar Motorcycles
Ongar (0277) 363236
Johns of Romford
Romford (0708) 26048/27069

GLOUCESTER
B.V.M. Moto
Stroud (045 36) 2743/2167

HAMPSHIRE
SPC Motorcycles
Aldershot (0252) 314011
Parkroad Motorcycles
(Southampton) Ltd
Southampton (0703) 228718

HEREFORD & WORCESTER
Mead & Tomkinson (Hereford)
Limited
Hereford (0432) 272341

HERTFORDSHIRE
Sawbridgeworth Motorcycles
(Hertford)
Hertford (0992) 53135

HUMBERSIDE
Eddy's Motorcycle Centre Ltd.
Hull (0482) 54252
Harveys
Laceby (0472) 71835

ISLE OF MAN
S & S Motors
Castletown (0624) 823 698

KENT
David Brown Motorcycles
(Ashford) Ltd
Ashford (0233) 27888/9
Normand Mobike Limited
Bromley (01) 851 4014
L & C Auto Services Limited
Tunbridge Wells (0892) 39355

LANCASHIRE
Keith Dixon Motorcycles
Accrington (0254) 31221
Doug Hacking Motorcycles
Bolton (0204) 491511
H. Robinson & Sons
Rochdale (0706) 45964

LEICESTERSHIRE
Evington Motorcycles Limited
Leicester (0533) 734242

LONDON
Park Lane Limited
Mayfair (01) 629 9277
Slocombes Limited
Neasden (01) 450 6644
Gus Kuhn Motors Limited
Stockwell (01) 733 1002
Hughes Motorcycles (S.H. Brand)
Limited
Tooting (01) 672 3077

MERSEYSIDE
Southport Superbike
Southport (0704)
36192/37480/38791

NOTTINGHAMSHIRE
Wheelcraft (Notts)
Nottingham (0602) 781432

OXFORDSHIRE
Hughenden M40 Ltd.
Milton Common (08446) 701/2

SALOP
Wylie & Holland
Market Drayton (0630) 57121

SHROPSHIRE
Church Stretton Motorcycle Centre
Church Stretton (0694) 723546

SOMERSET
Vincent & Jerrom
Taunton (0823) 72378

SUFFOLK
Revetts Limited
Ipswich (0473) 53726/7

SURREY
Coombs & Sons (Guildford) Limited
Guildford (0483) 502211

TYNE AND WEAR
Mill Garages Ltd
Sunderland (0783) 657631

W. MIDLANDS
Meadway Motorcycles
Birmingham (021) 783 6176
Godfrey Hall Ltd.
Coventry (0203) 591223
Cradley Heath Motorcycles
Cradley Heath (0384) 633455

WILTSHIRE
George White Motors
Swindon (0793) 22786/23519

YORKSHIRE
Carnell Motor Group
Doncaster (0302) 21383
Richardson Automotive
(Sheffield) Ltd
Sheffield (0742) 589432
Allan Jefferies Motorcycles
Shipley (0274) 587451
Barrie Robson Motorcycles
York (0904) 33479

B M W  K Series

CHANNEL ISLANDS

GUERNSEY
Jacksons Garage (Guernsey)
Limited
St Peter Port (0481) 35441

JERSEY
Jacksons Garage (Jersey) Limited
St Helier (0534) 20281/2/3

N. IRELAND

ANTRIM
Hurst Motorcycle Centre
Belfast (0232) 663632

SCOTLAND

GRAMPIAN
Shirlaws Garage
Aberdeen (0224) 584855

HIGHLAND
Calterdon Limited
Inverness (0463) 236566

LOTHIAN
Better Bikes Limited
Edinburgh (031) 667 9177

STRATHCLYDE
North Harbour Motorcycles
Ayr (0292) 281933
Scot Bike
Glasgow (041) 3341297

TAYSIDE
John Clark (Tayside) Limited
Dundee (0382) 815993

WALES

CLWYD
Tony's Cycles & Motorcycles
Prestatyn (07456) 3455

GWENT
South Wales Superbikes Ltd
Newport (0633) 859222

BMW (GB) Ltd
Ellesfield Avenud
Bracknell
Berks RG12 4TA
Telephone: (0344) 426565 (Head Office)
01-897 6665 (Literature Enquiries Only)
Telex: 849158

Index

B M W _____ K Series